AN INSIGHT

THE ICONIC BATTLE OF SARAGARHI

Echoes of the Frontier

EARLIER BOOKS BY THE AUTHOR

1. Ashes to Glory – The Saragarhi Battalion
2. As it Happened – Amazing Tell-Tales of Army Life
3. The Chameleons – The Gold Rush

AN INSIGHT

THE ICONIC BATTLE OF SARAGARHI

Echoes of the Frontier

Brig Kanwaljit Singh (Veteran)

UNITED SERVICE INSTITUTION OF INDIA
NEW DELHI

PENTAGON PRESS LLP

AN INSIGHT—THE ICONIC BATTLE OF SARAGARHI: Echoes of the Frontier

By Brig Kanwaljit Singh (Veteran)

First Published in 2018

ISBN 978-93-86618-60-3

Published by
PENTAGON PRESS LLP
206, Peacock Lane, Shahpur Jat
New Delhi-110049
Phones: 011-64706243, 26491568
Telefax: 011-26490600
email: rajan@pentagonpress.in
website: www.pentagonpress.in

Printed at Aegean Offset Printers, Greater Noida

DEDICATED TO

Those who martyred for the values they exemplified –
spirit of belief in righteousness of cause, redeeming honour,
inordinate valour and supreme sacrifice.

WORD

If you perform the sacrifice of doing duty, you do not have to do anything else. Devoted to duty, man attains perfection.

– Bhagwat Geeta

Contents

Afghanistan-Pakistan Border with Surrounding Countries

800909 (A05998) 9-88

THE BATTLE OF SARAGARHI

"On the Saragarhi ramparts died

The bravest of the brave.

Neath Saragarhi's ruined walls

They found a fitting grave.

For Saragarhi bears the fame

They gave their lives to save."

ICONIC - INDOMITABLE - UNPARALALLED - UNIQUE

PREFACE

An opportunity of immense value to pen down my account of the battle of Saragarhi fought on 12 September 1897, NWFP (Pakhtunwal), now in Pakistan, based on years of wide research and association with 4 Sikh (36th Sikhs or XXXVI of yore), arises at a juncture when there is flaming desire by many historians to rekindle interest in the battle. This illustrious battle has been described in various national and international forums, time and again, to most rousing acclaim through books, articles, presentations, videos and motion pictures

The aim of this book is to contextualise the situation, environment, tribulations, trends and transformations of the time so as to appreciate and comprehend the nature and necessity of skirmishes, battles and campaigns that took place in the 19th Century on the North West Frontier. The effort is to visualize the impact in an overall perspective. There is no pretention to project this book as a complete showcase of the history of NWFP, or even of a short contemporary period. It aims to present an overall appropriate, prudent and realistically pragmatic explanation keeping focus on the Battle of Saragarhi.

The truth of bravery can only be resolved by comprehending the ultimate veracity of it, including its inherent contradictions. Fortunately, for the seeker of historical actuality, this book endeavours to present just the right kind of information to puzzle out the nature of imagination, conjectures and irrelevance.

I have widened the arena of my study of the battle to include some extraneous aspects relevant to the cause, yet remaining within the orbit, basking in the glow of the glittering act of extreme bravery, dedication and sacrifice. This also is a consequential presentation to my earlier book "Saragarhi Battalion – Ashes to Glory" written in 1987, when I was fortunate to be the 36th Commanding Officer of this great Battalion on its Centenary.

A painting in abstracts of the battle scene was got made by me which also forms the jacket of the book mentioned. The original painting adorns the Officers' Messes 4 Sikh, Sikh Regimental Centre and Gurudawara Memorial at Ferozepur, it has now become world famous. Copies of it are displayed in all Sikh regiment units and numerous institutions.

The instability of the Frontiers was notorious because of the involvement of some adventurous nations, the audacious nature of the daring and exploratory military commanders and finally the locals, the tribesmen – the martial, independent nomad like clans, which were difficult to subdue. The Swat Valley was the flash point from where the simmering feeling of injustice transformed into an uprising that engulfed fertile lands of Samana, Tirah and Kurram. This then led the British to launch the most daring military campaign of enormous magnitude.

The numerous studies carried out, books and articles written, the government versions and war diaries do have contradictions, appeasements, distortions, parochialism or aspects of self boosting and ridiculing the adversary, which are understandable. Truth is truant defying search. In war it is shrouded being shy of overall picture, confusions, idealistic self aggrandizements of own actions and cloaking the performances of adversaries. Personal predilections and biases are embedded unconsciously or intentionally in the narratives. Sifting the truth requires deep research. While narrating the story here, exaggerations, as far as possible, have been kept at bay. The guiding principle has been to project a balanced view, though fully not feasible because of records of events that took place decades ago, and most written material available is by the British who were a party to the situation. However, it would be apt to add here words of Sir Olaf Caroe, K.C.S.I., K.C.I.E. that truer meaning of the skirmishes and wars brought out *'an affinity born out of a hundred wars of conflict, a mutual sense of honour, affection and esteem'*.

Though I had collected bits and pieces of the battle for years, the idea of writing an analysis germinated in 1965. After the capture of formidable Barki, Lahore Sector, on 10-11 September 1965, suffering heavy casualties, 4 Sikh, fighting continuously for six days without any respite, was selected for another daunting task in a totally new sector Khemkaran-Kasur, to establish a road block on 12 September, a Suitable commemoration of the Battle of Saragarhi.

An idea praiseworthy, but lacked the logic of foolproof intelligence, planning and coordination. The Unit carried out its mission most admirably and took up positions dominating the road to Kasur, but the formation failed to link up. A gallant bid was made but the devastating artillery fire and additional enemy armour to envelope the spread out groups, during day, caused many casualties. Some died fighting, some were able to extricate themselves, yet many were taken PoW. Lightly wounded, I was also captured. Destiny took us to PoW Camps established in forts of bygone era, at Kohat and Dargai. We could see the Samana Ridge where our predecessors had fought a magnificent battle in the truest sense of 'last man last round'. The impalpable nostalgic mixes of feelings were incomprehensible.

My interest in this epitome of bravery was rewarded when as Commandant the Sikh Regimental Centre at Ramgarh, Bihar, an imposing Memorial was made in 1992 which was inaugurated by Lieutenant General P S Vadehra, PVSM, the ex Colonel of the Regiment. It is located alongside the magnificent building of the 'Museum and Motivation Hall' which was constructed during 1992-1994, where some artifacts of Saragarhi are displayed proudly.

Lieutenant General Kirpal Singh Randhawa, PVSM, AVSM, had given a presentation on the Battle of Saragarhi at Delhi on 11 September 2005, immediately after his exploring visits to the scene of the battle. I along with some stalwarts and serving officers of the 4 Sikh had attended the same and had been able to gain information of ground realities.

A summary of history and glorious achievements of 4 Sikh is given in a separate chapter which showcases the indomitable spirit of Saragarhi.

I am prodded today to explain the epochmaking battle as an analyzed analogy. Details already available in some great books and writings, not explanatory to the Battle of Saragarhi or not adding to the stature of people who fought at Frontiers, Samana or Tirah have been considered inconsequential and thus have been ignored. My effort has been to take essence of gigantic records available, understand the formidable authentic or derived narrations and present to the reader 'why', 'how' and 'what next'. The focus thus would be on the events of 1890s, with of course an essential background of circumstances and the people involved to make a wholesome objective study.

The numerous maps and sketches in books of by gone eras are illustrative. They have been, as such, included by the writers of today and placed in their books and articles suitably and amicably. I have, however, taken the liberty of combining some sketches which are more explanatory, vivid and easy to comprehend. This exercise also reduces the number of sketches so required otherwise to explain the situations and events.

For decades efforts have been afoot to locate descendents of the Saragarhi martyrs. A few of them have been in touch with 4 Sikh and attended Saragarhi Day celebrations, at Ferozepur or at the Sikh Regimental Centre. One more family has been located recently. Whereabouts of almost 11 are still not available, in spite of several attempts through newspapers and intense search in villages that were recorded at the time of recruitment of the martyrs. I invite information about those yet not found.

I have also added some interesting themes 'tactics', 'last stand', 'why soldiers fight', 'why Indians fought the British battles', 'jurisprudence of Durand Line' and some 'determinants' of the time to present it as essentials for an analysis.

Colonel H.D. Hutchison wrote on 01 September 1898: "*... when I write the story of a campaign, endeavoured to state so much of the facts which are notorious as many enable the general reader to form his own conclusions as to the cause of the war and " what they killed each other for.*"

> *"Now tell us all about the war,*
> *And what they killed each other for?*
> *"Why, that I cannot tell, 'said he',*
> ***"but 't was a famous victory!"***

Brig Kanwaljit Singh (Veteran)

MESSAGE

The Saragarhi battle occupies a special status as it was a saga of unparalleled bravely in which valiant soldiers of 36th Sikh Regiment faced the onslaught of 10,000 Afridis and Orakzai tribes on Sunday 12th Sept., 1897 at Saragarhi post.

The Pathans knew that, just like them, the Sikhs too, were invincible and brave, who during the rule of Maharaja Ranjit Singh, had defeated them. General Hari Singh Nalwa (Pride of Khalsa) had crushed them on their soil, the Khalsa insignia was raised in the region from Jamrod Fort to Attuk River.

The unique battle started on Sunday morning at 9am and continued until 4pm. In keeping with the Call of Duty and the Sikh tradition of valour in battle, each and every soldier died in hand to hand combat, only after killing and wounding hundreds of Pathans.

One British soldier J.A. Lindsay of the relief party on 14th September after Saragarhi Post was regained, said, "Around 400 Pathan bodies were found and also 21 Sikhs who were martyred at Saragarhi Post, ...The detachment of the 36th Sikhs marched over from Gulistan this morning (Sept, 14th) carrying the standards they had captured from the enemy, they are a splendid corps and have made a great name for themselves".

The battle was over; it entered the annals that are a tribute to the human spirit. My colleague historian Brig. Kanwaljit Singh wrote a book, "Saragarhi Battalion: Ashes to Glory" in 1987 the centenary year of 4 Sikh. This present book is testament to the efforts of Sardar Kanwaljit Singh to bring the iconic Battle of Saragarhi to Life.

Gurinderpal Singh Josan
Sikhsinamerica@gmail.com
001-516-885-7758
New York, U.S.A.

GENERAL BIPIN RAWAT
UYSM, AVSM, YSM, SM; ADC

MESSAGE

An Indian soldier is recognized and admired world over, for his resilience, stern sense of responsibility, utmost valour and when need arises, remains steadfast, never hesitating to lay down his life, in accomplishing his mission. His astute understanding of the cause, utter belief in faith and following the traditions and rich ethos set by the predecessors is exemplary. He stands out for his stout will, determination and devotion to duty.

The Battle of Saragarhi was enacted in the same unconquerable spirit. It is a quintessence of bravery and sacrifice. A well bound small team of determined soldiers under the awe-inspiring leadership of Havildar Ishar Singh, fought tenaciously against thousands, sure of death, yet defied it in utter belief in duty. The Battle is a true epitome of selflessness for a cherished cause. The names of such martyrs shall remain forever etched in the annals of history.

My heart swelled with pride as I went through each chapter of the saga of Guts and Glory, so well compiled through, 'An Insight - The Iconic Battle of Saragarhi - Echoes of the Frontier', written by Brigadier Kanwaljit Singh. His vast research, collection of factual data and putting it across lucidly is highly creditable. The pitch, substance and appreciation of the situation is commendable.

'Jai Hind'

(Bipin Rawat)
General

Lt Gen SK Jha, PVSM, AVSM, YSM, SM
Colonel of The Sikh Regiment

MESSAGE

At the very outset, I as **Colonel of the most decorated Regiment of the Indian Army** take this opportunity to express our homage to gallant martyrs and gratitude to our veterans. Each and every battalion of the Regiment has excelled in all the professional fields, bringing the Regiment to a threshold of pinnacles of achievements and glory. Our ethos of dedication, valour and sacrifice is imbibed from the teachings of our Gurus and predecessors who guided and upheld the cause majestically. We take pride in our past and vow to keep up our National 'Nishan' - **'THE TRICOLOUR'** ever flying mightiest.

The invincible **'Battle of Saragarhi'** is enshrined in the ethos of the Regiment. It is an epitome that we rever, the glowing achievement of a handful of our forerunners who withstood thousands, defying, terrible odds and a far concluded death living upto our motto:

'Deh shiva bar money ehai
Shubh karman te kabhun na taron,
Nah darun arison jab jaye laron
Nische kar apni jeet karon'

Our Regimental stalwart, a battle veteran, Brigadier Kanwaljit Singh, has written an analysis of the Battle, elucidating the whole gamut of soldiering, bringing out a book that glorified the basic edifice of spirit of fighting and sacrifice to the cause. I find the book revealing, engrossing and stirring.

I wish him the very best of luck for his future endeavours.

"WAHEGURU JI KA KHALSA, WAHEGURU JI KI FATEH"

(SK Jha)
Lieutenant General
Colonel of The Sikh Regiment

MESSAGE

The study of Indian military history affords us many examples of valour and devotion over and above the call of duty but few can surpass the gallantry displayed by the small band of men of the erstwhile 36th Sikhs (now 4 Sikh)at Saragarhi during the great Frontier Uprising of 1897.

Faced with overwhelming odds these 21 men chose death over dishonour and fell fighting to the last man and the last bullet. In doing so they exemplified the military ethos of the Indian soldier through the ages. By their sacrifice they have left behind a legacy of *Nishkama Dharma* for others to emulate.

The author of this book has done a great service by his endeavour to highlight the events of the iconic battle of Saragarhi and to place it in the larger context of the history of his battalion. He has painstakingly collected an immense amount of information for the elucidation and education of his readers. I am sure his efforts to generate awareness of this historic battle and the valour and ethos of the men who fought in it will be crowned with success and that the legacy of Saragarhi will endure within the Sikh Regiment and the Indian Army.

Sqn Ldr Rana TS Chhina (Retd)
Secretary and Editor
Centre for Armed Forces Historical Research
United Service Institution of India

ACKNOWLEDGEMENTS

At the outset, I wish to acknowledge with my utmost thanks the eminent United Service Institution of India for their magnanimity for accepting my book for editing and publishing it under their aegis.

My extreme gratitude is to General Bipin Rawat, UYSM, AVSM, YSM, SM, VSM; ADC, Chief of the Army Staff, for his benevolent 'Message' for the Book, appreciating the human spirit of Indian soldier and his tribute to the martyrs.

I gratefully acknowledge with special thanks to Lieutenant General S K Jha, PVSM, AVSM, YSM, SM, Colonel of the Sikh Regiment for his sterling support and a befitting 'Message' for the Book.

I acknowledge appreciations by eminent historians Squadron Leader Rana T S Chhina, MBE, and Mr G S Josan and having been kind to write 'Messages'.

The records available in the 4th Battalion The Sikh Regiment have been of immense value. I thank Colonels G R Sharma, V K Sheoran and S K Ninama, for providing access to the records. I also wish to express thankful appreciation to Colonel P P S Virk and Captain A S Jaijee who have provided me materials they had collected during their service with 4 SIKH. Thanks are also due to young Priya Negi who did graphics for me.

I feel proud to having attended 'Presentations' by Late Lieutenant General K S Randhawa, PVSM, AVSM, Mister Gurinderpal Singh Josan, a historian from USA and Captain Jay Sohal from UK, where they brought out significant facts.

Professor Ranjit Singh and Doctor Bhupinder Singh, both splendid writers, have very kindly gone through my script and extended suggestions of immense value. I extend my grateful thanks to them.

Research, collecting inputs from several resources, and penning the same has taken long time, bringing seriousness in my demeanour and non-availability to home deliverances, which have been endured by the entire family, my wife Manmeet, son Mandeep (a 4 SIKH officer, third generation army background), daughter in law Sarneet, son in law Joaquim, daughter Sonam, and especially the grandchildren Mehak, Ishan and Chez. They were also generously forthcoming with their ideas and valuable suggestions. I wish to thank them for their fortitude, cooperation and inspiration.

I am deeply indebted to Lieutenant General P K Singh, PVSM, AVSM, Major General P K Goswami, VSM and Squadron Leader Rana T S Chhina, MBE, of USI, for ensuring the script in best form. My thanks are due to Lieutenant General Ian Cardozo, AVSM, SM, for going through the manuscript and suggesting amendments to make it presentable.

Lastly, I must thank with whole hearted admiration Pentagon Press for painstakingly editing and publishing the Book in the best possible form to be proud of.

Brig Kanwaljit Singh (Veteran)

CHAPTER ONE

ECHOES OF THE FRONTIER

General

The Battle of Saragarhi was fought on 12 September 1897 on Samana Ridge, in the Khanki Valley, Tirah, in North West Frontier Province (NWFP), of the then India, and now in Pakistan. To understand the rationale and circumstances that led to this battle, it would be essential to understand the topography and climate since these influenced the adversaries and military operations immensely. Those who participated in battles at Tirah were from different regions, races, and creeds. They varied in physique, characteristics, and abilities. The geographical features of the Frontiers had a mammoth effect on their strategy, tactics, and logistics. The field was wild, difficult, large and unknown that involved the Indian Forces into a serious war. The name NWFP itself conjures up illusory perceptions.

Neighbouring Countries. The immediate neighbour to the NWFP is Afghanistan – a country which has international borders with three countries viz; Russia in the North, Iran (then Persia/Prussia) in the West, and India in the South-East. During the nineteenth century, Afghanistan was a buffer between the British India and Russia. *Today, the Frontiers form part of Pakistan as a Federally Administered Tribal Area (FATA) and Baluchistan. FATA consists of seven semi-autonomous agencies or administrative units – Khyber, Mohmand, Bajaur, Kurram, Orakazai, North Waziristan and South Waziristan – all mountainous areas. Baluchistan, a sandy vast area is South of FATA.*

NWFP. The NWFP is like a triangle, its North-West edge being at Zulfikar and from there the line lies along Russia North-Eastwards leading to the River Oxus (Amu) at Khamiab. Northwards, this river forms no obstacle for movement most of the year. In its South, lies a narrow strip of Afghan territory like a panhandle, south of which the boundary between British India and Afghanistan lay. It was a buffer between the two empires. This thus was the main approach taken by the invaders to Afghan Turkistan. The river then reaches its Eastern end to Lake Victoria, from where the Frontier runs to the Pamirs which have snow most of the year. The border line from there crosses into Sinkiang, a Chinese province. From this point a line was drawn on 12 Nov 1893, which demarcated the alignment between Afghanistan and the NWFP. It is about 1500 miles (2430 KM) long border that was signed between Sir Mortimer Durand for British India and Akbar Rahman Khan, the Afghan Amir. This line depicted spheres of influence between the two. Afghanistan was accepted as an independent country but with a proviso that its foreign affairs and diplomatic relations would be controlled by the British.

The line from Zulfikar moves South for 600 miles, towards Persia, then South-East and further South to the Arabian Sea.

The North-West border of the NWFP runs along the Southern edge of the intruding finger of Afghanistan territory for about 200 miles to Chitral and Wakhan, where it is only nine miles across.

Westwards from Khamiab, the borders run across rough areas of steppes and desert. Then North-East, it follows a rugged wild line through a long stretch of rocky mountains, keeping Suleiman Ranges in the North. The line then moves Southwards towards Waziristan, and then to Sufed Koh which dominates Kurram and Khaiber by observation.

From the North-East of Wakhan, is the Hindu Kush, 600 miles long, with peaks touching 19,000 feet and above, which separates North and Central Asia from Southern Asia. It is an extremely tough country full of precipitous gorges and gushing rivers. South Westwards, the range joins into Sufed Koh. The border then runs along the valleys formed by the River Kabul, heads Eastwards along the River Kunar, hugging West of Chitral ending at the Hindu Kush in Wakhan, from where formidable mountainous terrain continues astride the Kabul River towards Herat.

In the South-Western areas from Kabul, there are the Hazara Highlands, then stony mountains descending into deserts of Kandhar. Rivers Farah Rud, Helmand and Arghandab flow into marshes and salt laden lakes on the Persian border.

It is essential to appreciate the peculiarities, difficulties, and opportunities offered by the vast, difficult, and treacherous terrain. The tough area of NWFP had afflicted the locals to be a hardened people as much by the invaders from across Afghanistan, who influenced their psyche to become stubborn opposition, and a natural aptness to warfare to accept no sovereign – foreign or from among themselves. Many invaders crossed these tracts to reach India, to name some – Alexander of Macedonia, Qutaybs ibn Muslim, Mahmoud Ghazni, Ghengis Khan, Timur, Babur and Ahmad Shah Durrani. It would, therefore, be important to understand various approaches available in the region.

Routes of Ingress

In the South, Makran formed a crucial landing harbour to invaders, from where the trade routes to India emanated. These routes were however subject to blinding sand storms driven by high winds. The road Herat – Kandhar-Indian Frontier at Chaman – Quetta – Bolan – Sibi or Harnai – Loralai – Zhob Valley – Gomal, about 600 miles, was no easy thoroughfare. The distance from Herat to Kandhar is 360 miles; and from Kandhar to Chaman 60 miles. From Herat to the Russian frontier post and rail head at Kushak it is 60 miles, where it crosses Kohe Sufed. Here the heights are only 5000 feet. These routes from North of Hindu Kush to Kabul for traders and invaders were easy comparatively, and thus were in much use. The two routes from Kabul, one running South of Sufed Koh towards Kurram Valley, and another along River Kabul to Khyber Pass to Peshawar were the best and most favoured.

Also there are approaches from Badakashan over the Hindu Kush into Chitral via the Nuksan and Dorah passes. These are at a height of 14,500 feet. Though winters were severe, making trekking difficult and hazardous, these were used even in winter for pack animals for trading wood and cloth merchandise Westwards, and fire arms and cutlery Eastwards. Approaches to India from North were easier than vice versa. The movement from the Russian Post Osh, descending about 70 miles to the Indian frontier allowed rapid advance. The elevation of Chitral is about 5000 feet. The climate is Meditterranen with warm summers and cold winters. There also was the advantage of vast green pastures that helped in logistics. This obviously was the crux that provided fodder to possibilities of a Russian venture to India, a nightmarish suspense in the British psyche.

From North to South, the tribal areas of concern were Chitral, Kohistan, Bajur, Tirah, Waziristan and Baluchistan (to be reconciled with today's Pakistan's FATA and Baluchistan).

The vagaries differed vigorously on each route for trade or invasion.

(a) In the North, through the Vakhan corridor, across passes Mandal, Nuksan and Dorah, through Chitral, is the shortest to the Frontiers and hence to India. The hills are low. But the roads and tracks were tough as they were not fully developed. These were used by the Russian and Chinese traders.

(b) From Russia and Iran, via Herat to Kabul, crossing from the Khyber Pass to Peshawar. It was the best route hence the most frequented by traders or invaders.

(c) The approaches across North of Hindu Kush to Kabul were comparatively easy and also direct. These were in fair use.

(d) Herat to Kandhar – Quetta and to Frontiers, both North eastwards and South eastwards. Area West of Kandhar was extremely difficult.

(e) From South Arabian Sea to Makran, Arab traders and some invaders used this route.

The Tirah

Coming closer to the Frontier, Tirah, also called Tirah Valley, stretches from the Khyber Pass to Kurram constituting 700 square miles. It is a stretchy geographical elucidation of hills that somewhat look like the back of a hand – knuckles, fingers and spaces. It has several valleys which have the Bara River as a source. From the Sufed Koh, to its South-East is the Rajgul Valley, through which flows a tributary of the Bara, flowing South towards the Mastura and Khanki rivers, to Kurram, forming an obstacle to any invasion. The basin is of rich alluvial soil since filled up with detritus brought by the rivers turning the valleys most fertile. Slopes are terraced, riveted and irrigated. The important valleys are Maidan, Rajgul, Waran, Bara and Mastura. Approaches along these rivers, starting from Kurramare direct without need to cross any pass, but are very difficult to move because of the lay of the land, numerous narrow defiles and necessity of crossing the rivers again and again. Making of roads along the rivers was a nightmare. All highlands South and Eastwards from the watershed of the

Sufed Koh range were inhabited by Afridis and Orakazais. Westwards, the area was inhabited by Chamkanis and Masozais.

The other directions to venture into Tirah were either from the North or South, both requiring crossing of the passes. There were difficulties of climbing up the steep slopes and dislodging the enemy from the hilltops, but the move down was easy into the lush green valleys with abundance of local resources. From the South, the start could be from the post of Shinwari, and across main passes of Chagru (5525 feet) near Dargai, connecting Miranzai and Khanki Valleys, the Sampagha (6550 feet), leading from Khanki to Mastura Valley, and the Arhanga (7050 feet), separating Masture valley from Maidan, Saransar (8650 feet), leads from Maidan into Bara Valley, the Tseri Kandao (8575 feet) separates Maidan from Waran Valley and the Sapri Pass (5190 feet) leads from East of Mastura Valley to the Bara Valley. The routes were extremely narrow and posed terrible problems to move of animal transport which numbered in thousands. The few open areas were within effective range of a rifle from the hills. Shinwari was an area originally under the British. It overlooked Miranzai and partially the Kurram Valley.

Sampagha Pass is a very conspicuous knoll where the Orakazais had made 'sangars' to fight from, and when in danger the defenders fled to the shadowed cracks and natural caves. Move down from there, about 700 feet or so was easy. At Arahanga Pass, the Afridis had not made any 'sangars' to fight from. The descent from there to the Maidan Plain was about 1000 feet. It is an oval shaped valley, about eight miles long and four miles wide. For years the debris that flowed down from the hills into this valley has made the land most fertile. There were long stretches of terraced fields towards Bagh. There were fruit trees of walnut, mulberry and apricot dotted all around. The houses were square, flat topped and two storied, made of timber and mud. The house of the Mullah, Sayed Akbar of Waran, was the best, where stone had been used. The tribal *'jirgahs'* (assemblies) were held at Bagh.

Movement through the valleys required recognition of hill tops that needed to be secured and picqueted.

Khyber is the crucial point that connects Central Asia, Afghanistan and India. This was on the route most significant of all the approaches, an absolute necessity to be kept open for carrying out trade. This, significantly, was the home of the Afridis and Orakazais.

The Climate

The climate ranges between two extremes. In the northern gigantic mountains, the cold is excruciating. The temperatures are minus degrees in winters, affecting closing of the passes. The frightening winds at great speeds lash out with immense punitive ferociousness.

In the South, there are hot deserts, where blistering sandstorms cause havoc to a moving column. The sand-dunes restrict free movement. There is acute shortage of water and vegetation. The dwellings are far and widely spaced. The high temperatures in summers and the extreme cold in winters are agonizing. The logistic support to any force of reasonable size is mind-boggling.

The tribal houses, in the East, being on the knife sharp ridges, were inhospitable. These, however, were interspersed with beautiful valleys that had cool streams, rivulets and rivers that irrigate lavishly rich terraced fields that grow crops, fruit trees and timber. These provided shelter. Hundreds of animals that carried the baggage of the columns could be fed with ease. In the rainy season, movement became terribly cumbersome as it became invariably extremely cold and forces had to survive without much clothing. The rivers swelled causing disruptions to movement. This however suited the light footed Afghans as they could survive the rigours comparatively with ease.

Bara Valley is ten by four miles with heights ranging to 5000 feet. While in winters this valley is fairly comfortable, in summers it gets very hot. East of Maidan is Wapran Valley, about same size as above. The Bara Valley that stretches towards Peshawar has in its north the Bazar Valley, with heights ranging between 5000 to 20000 feet. In summers the Afridis used to move to the cool of Maidan. To its South is Mastura Valley at a height of 6000 feet and next to it is the Miranzai Valley.

Inhabitation

Bara valley was inhabited by Kuki Khel Afridis; Zakka Khels in Bazar Valley, Wapran Valley and Mamanai area. Maidan and Mastura Valleys had Adam Khels. South of Arhanga Pass were Orakazais. Area of Dargai had Rabbia Khels; Thal, Hangu and Kohat had Khattaks. Kurram was inhabited by Chamkanis, to its East were Massozais and further were Mamuzais till Dargai. It would be of interest that the Chamkanis, Massozais and Mamuzais, though similar to others in all their persona did not consider themselves to be Afghans.

Historical and Political Perspective: In Nutshell

The Durand Line, significantly the line of discord, runs into areas inhabited by Pashtuns who are living there for centuries. Arabs had conquered these areas in the 7th Century. They introduced Islam. Some of them settled down in these parts. These areas were trespassed by several traders, invaders and despots viz., Ghaznis, Gauris (Ghurids), Taimurs, Mughals (Mongols), Hotakis, Khiljis, Lodhis, Uzbeks, Greeks, Tajilks and Durranis. They came through Afghanistan, conquering areas of interest, reorganizing their armies to march East for gold and ivory in the land of elephants, peacocks and apes – India. They marched through the Frontiers, with tacit and sometimes active support of the locals. However, we shall concentrate on the period of our interest i.e., nineteenth century.

Ahmad Shah Durrani is regarded as the founder of Afghanistan. Later, Amanullah Khan, the Amir of Afghanistan, was able to follow an independent foreign policy. At the time of Russo-British intrigue in the 18th Century, Amir Dost Mohammad, and on his death, his son Akbar Barkazai ruled Afghanistan. Then Amir Abdul Rahman Khan, grandson of Dost Mohammad ruled from 1880 to 1901, a period of main interest of this study.

Maharaja Ranjit Singh, with a judicious mixture of diplomacy and force wielded a viable strong kingdom – Punjab. The drums of the Sikh empire resonated from Sutlej to Khyber and from Ladakh to Sindh, one of the largest kingdoms of Hindu India. He subdued tribes of Abbottabad, fought a magnificent battle at Nowshera. He received tributaries from the local Barakazai rulers. Dost Mohammad attacked Jamrud twice but was defeated by the Sikhs under Maharaja Ranjit Singh's finest General Hari Singh Nalwa. The British interest in these areas had already taken root.

In 1849, after annexation of the Sikh territories, the British Indian forces initiated the First Anglo-Afghan War, which was an utter disaster. Their effort to place Shah Shuja on the throne of Afghanistan could not be sustained by them. In 1978-80, the British fought the Second Anglo-Afghan War and succeeded in acquiring some geographical objectives. Treaty of Gandamak, 26 May, 1879, forced the Amir to cede control of designated frontier territories to the British Empire. The diplomatically drawn Durand Line created the province of NWFP.

Why did the British evince such great interest in the Frontiers and Afghanistan? The latter had strategic significance since it was a buffer state between Imperial Russia and India. The Russian interest lay in Central Asia and the British in South Asia. The Russians had supported Iran to capture Herat, the Western gateway to India. The British otherwise had nothing to fear from Afghanistan or Iran but were apprehensive of Russian overtures in the area. The two Anglo-Afghan Wars were meant to have control on these areas against an assumed Tsarist Russian invasion, thus playing the *'Great Game'* as it came to be known. There were stories hovering around that a phantom Russian Army was moving South across the Kazakh steppes. Undoubtedly, the British, to an extent, over estimated this external threat.

It had to be till 1895 that the doubts remained, then the matters between the two were settled after numerous meeting and agreements. The Wakhan Corridor became part of Afghanistan as a no man's land between Russia and British controlled areas.

Here it must be understood that the Pashtoon areas though were invaded by numerous armies of repute, but were never totally subjugated. Assorted armies passed through these wild areas, tried to take control and administer the Frontier, but were never successful in acclaiming total sovereignty. At best, the Pashtoons were forced into coalitions, treaties, and promises which they violated with impunity. The British were also not able to disarm them totally and administer the Tirah area, except for few more accessible tribes. These areas thus remained free, untaxed, and unadministered.

The indomitable passion that the invaders possessed venturing from their home lands of Persia, Arabian countries, Russia and China to move hundreds of miles calls for acceptance of their zeal for adventure. Notwithstanding the circumstances of the time whether in their own countries or conditions prevailing in places far off or to satisfy lure and lust for fortunes, to assuage egos or endeavor adventures, they displayed enthusiasm, bravery and sacrifice. Success or failure of the invader or defender was all in the making of history of the human spirit.

In such a bid, therefore, in January 1839, Lord Auchinleck, Governor general of India decided to venture against Afghanistan and initiated first Anglo-Afghan War via Kandhar to Kabul to reinstate Shah Shuja as Amir at Kabul. The Sikhs were also to advance via Khyber to Kabul but did not because Maharaja Ranjit Singh fell sick. Before this, two brothers Shah Zaman and Shah Shuja were dethroned in turn, and in 1810 a third brother, Shah Mahmud became king of Afghanistan. But the real power was with the Wazir Futteh Khan and with Barkazai Mohammed Azim, and his three brothers Yar Mohmmed, Sultan Mohammed and Dost Mohammad. The campaign proved to be an utter disaster. The British then adopted a policy of 'Masterly Inactivity'. In 1878-80, the British launched the Second Anglo-Afghan War. This was also prompted due to Russian advance to the Amu Darya. The British succeeded in achieving some geographical objectives. They adopted a more aggressive 'Forward Policy'. Treaty of Gandamak, 26 May 1879, dictated the ceding of control of designated frontiers territories to the British Empire. The diplomatically drawn Durand Line in 1893, created the province of NWFP. These areas included Multan, Mianwali, Bahawalpur and Dera Ghazi Khan (the erstwhile Durrani Empire, 1709 to 1820), and then under Sikh Empire. The demarcation was along distinct ridge lines, rivers or through the boundary pillars that were erected. Permanent touch with the Frontier was concluded and constant alertness was created through placement of a special force called the Punjab Frontier Force (PFF). The British began improving roads and laying railway line.

The Afghans resented this ingress. In July 1897, they killed the British Political Agent at Tochi. They followed it with aggression against the Khyber forts. British garrisons at Malakand and Chakdara were attacked. By August, the Mohammad tribesmen attacked Shabqadr; Afridis and Orakazais invested Tirah and the Khyber Pass. The famous Battle of Saragarhi was a result of this Afghan resurgence.

Treaties and Agreements

A number of agreements were signed between the British, Amir and the tribesmen. Several letters and documents were found during Tirah Campaign which had resulted in a turbulent situation. A summary of documents is given in succeeding paragraphs. **(Full texts of letters and documents leading to upheaval are omitted.)**

Treaty between Amir Dost Mohammad Khan and British India, 30th March 1855. The treaty was signed by the representatives of both the parties at Peshawar. The essentials of three articles of the Treaty were a wish for perpetual peace and friendship, respect to territories in possession of each party and the Amir to treat enemies and friends of East India Company as such.

Agreement between Afghanistan and British India against Persian Aggression, 26th January, 1857. This treaty was signed at Peshawar. It aimed to checkmate the Shah of Persia who had taken possession of Herat, from any further advance towards the territories of Amir. The East India Company agreed to provide one lakh rupees monthly to Amir to raise and maintain 18,000 troops, cavalry and infanty, who would be under constant scrutiny by the British representatives at Kabul or Kandhar or Balakh or at all the three places or wherever an Afghan army assembled to act against the Persians. The representatives would only oversee and not interfere in the internal affairs of Kabul. The British agreed to overlook earlier hostilities of all tribes of Afghanistan and to provide 4000 additional muskets to already given 4000. Further clarification on earlier agreements and additional conditions were drawn to have cordial relations and record incidents of any violation.

Agreement fixing Afghanistan's Northern Frontier. The Agreement was signed on 12 November 1893, whereby River Oxus was to form the Northern Boundary of Afghanistan as decided between the Governments of Russia and England. The boundary was from Lake Victoria on the East to the junction of Kokcha with the Oxus. It was undertaken that all districts North of Oxus shall be the property of Russia and South of it that of Afghanistan. Any districts held by any party contrary to above, shall be transferred to the party so decided upon.

Treaty of Gandomak: Mohammed Jamal Hanifi, 26 May 1879. As answer to the uncalled for visit of a Russian delegation to Kabul on 22 July 1878, the British planned a mission to Kabul, which was denied entry to Afghanistan. It was considered an insult. The British declared war and moved a force to Kurram Valley, Peiwar Pass, then via Khyber Pass and Quetta towards Jallalabad and Kandhar. Amir Sher Ali Khan moved towards Russia to seek help but died near Balkh. His son Mohammed Yakub took over. He signed the Treaty of Gandomak under which he surrendered foreign affairs of Afghanistan to the British. The treaty also permitted increase in trade and placement of a British Mission in Kabul. But the Amir's unsatisfied troops stormed the mission on 03 September

1879 and massacred all the personnel, which forced the British to launch their Second Anglo Afghan War and made Mohammed Yakub's expulsion and placement of his cousin Abdur Rehman as Amir of Afghanistan. The British agent was to have all Indian Muslims as his staff at Kabul. The treaty was 'the most humiliating ever signed by an Afghan ruler' making the Afghan ruler a 'virtually feudatory of the British Crown'.

Treaty of Gandomak, 1879. The agreement was signed along with the above for perpetual peace. Its contents allowed the Amir's subjects to have dealings with the British, he would seek advice and concurrence of the British for foreign affairs and whenever British military intervention was required, all help would be given. The British would have a representative at Kabul and wherever required, would be protected by the Amir's forces. Facilities for mutual trade would be created, which included a telegraph line. Kandhar and Jallalabad were returned to the Amir, while the British had the control of districts of Kurram, Pishin and Sibi. The British also retained control of Khyber and Michni Passes. The British agreed to pay annual subsidy for Amir's assistance.

Letter from Sir Mortimer Durand to Amir Abdul Rehman Khan, dated 11 November, 1893. It was to confirm the contents of letter written earlier by Mr Griffin to the Amir. It clarified that if any foreign power interfered in the internal affairs of Afghanistan, the British Government would aid the Amir to such extent and in a manner to repel it, provided Amir abided by advice of the British Government in regard to external affairs. It reiterated the necessity to demarcate the border with Russia to eradicate any doubt ensuring security.

Agreement fixing Afghanistan's Northern Frontier, 12 November 1893. It was to reiterate letter of 11 November 1893.

The Durand Line Agreement, 12 November 1893. The Durand line was a 1510 miles (2430 kilometers) long border drawn between Afghanistan and NWFP, signed between Amir of Afghanistan and Sir Mortimer Durand, the British Representative, to fix the relative spheres of influence aiming to improve inter-relations. It was a single page document of seven articles. Demarcation was done for 800 miles and clarified the country of Afghanistan as a buffer zone between Russia and the British India. The line had cut through Pashtun and Baluch areas with dangerous portends geographic and geostrategic. The British agreed to double the annual subsidy to the Amir.

It was a dagger in the simmering feelings of the Pathans that drew them drastically to an edge of aggression. That resulted into punitive exercises, an enormous campaign by the then master adventurers, the British.

Agreement on the Sphere of Influence between Russia and Great Britain 1895. It was a clarification in the region of Pamirs; from Lake Victoria towards Chinese territories, and towards Hindukush. It was to implement the agreement between Russia, Great Britain and Afghanistan, with the spirit of 'give and take', and agreement to evacuate certain positions for the benefit of the other or for neutrality.

This thus is the summary of the events of countries and areas involved, rationale of ventures and outcome that the contestants brought about.

NORTH WEST FRONTIER PROVINCE

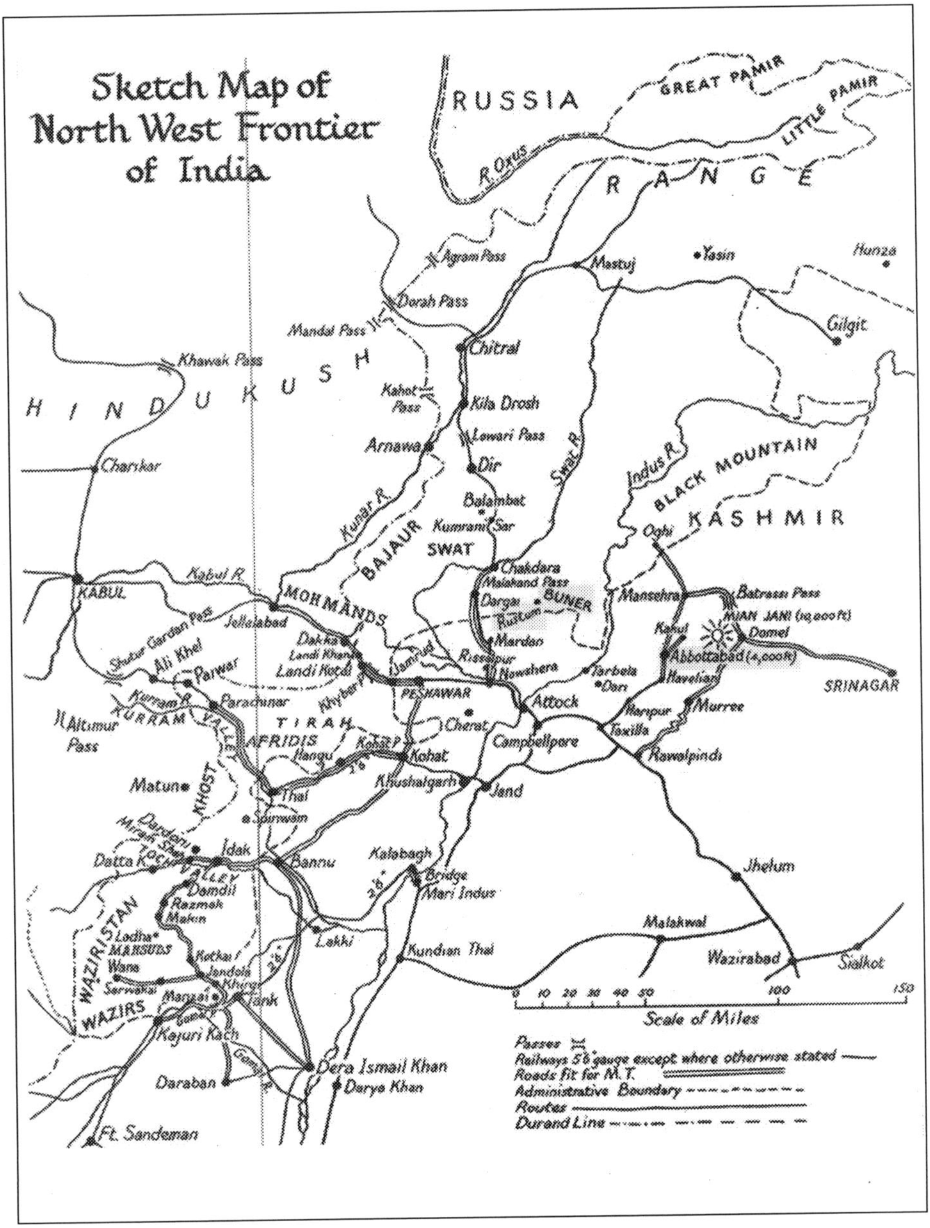

CHAPTER TWO

FRONTIER TRIBES (1890s and before)

"...If you know your enemy, you need not fear the result of a hundred battles."

General

The tribesmen of the Frontiers were a conglomeration of races admirably experienced in battles and wars, their history dating back to about five centuries BC. Their lands were formidable, varied and indomitable. They had adopted Islam when the Arabs had attacked them. Some go back in history to hypothesize that they were the lost ten tribes of Israel, customs being identical. There were several tribes that abounded in those areas, the primary ones being, from North to South, the Afridis, Yousefzais, Orakazais and Sadoji.

Tribesmen – who?

Who is an Afghan, Pathan, Pashtoon, Pakhtoon or Pushtun? Agreeably, these are alternate names of the same offshoot. They are traditional pastoral nomads, (herders who have frequently moved to find grazing lands). The kingdom of Afghanistan, believed to be founded by Ahmad Shah Durrani, is a hotchpotch of many tribes formed by mixed nationalities drawn from different regions of Asia. Some claim descent from the Arabs, the Sayyids, and descendants of Muhammad. There are other groups around Peshawar and Kandhar who claim descendance from the Greeks when Alexander who had attacked in 330 BC. The Afghans are a majority. They claim to be of Israeli descent. Most inhabitants of NWFP are Afghans. Since they all claim to be from 'Durrani' heritage, which forms the rationale of common religion and language, thus a brotherhood. The Amir (Ameer), the King of Afghanistan, was their religious head.

The Pathans are the ones who speak Pashto, the language of Afghanis, they all thus are Pathans, who are settled Southwards from Amu Darya up to West of Indus River, also applies to those tribes living in the Frontier. They have a faith of having been born from the seed of Abraham. The tribes were independent, never subjugated by the Amirs who had been trying to do so. Yet a dispute between tribal *'Jirgas'* was referred to their spiritual head, the Amir. The British interest lay in a division between Afghanistan and area from there to the Indian borders, laid by the Sikhs, under Maharaja Ranjit Singh.

Divergent Views

Different views have been advanced about the Pathans by military leaders and British envoys. Perspective by Mountstuart Elphinstone seems to be a balanced projection: *'Their vices are revenge, envy, avarice, rapacity and obstinacy; on the other hand, they are fond of liberty, faithful to their friends, kind to their dependents, hospitable, brave, hardy, frugal, laborious and prudent'.* Ironically, he adds further: *'Ruthless, cowardly robberies, cold-blooded, treacherous murder, are in to him the salt of life. Brought up from his earliest childhood amid scenes of appalling treachery and merciless revenge, nothing can ever change him. As he lived – 'shameless cruel savage – so he dies'.* Some historians have also pointed out that pathans resorted to castration, mutilation and skinning.

The writers, mostly Western, have painted tribesmen as savage, ruthless, remorseless, undependable, frisky, turbulent, and rebellious. Colonel C. E. Collwell describes them as *'marauding cut-throats, exceptionally fine mountaineers, admirable marksmen and ferocious adversaries'*. Even during the reign of Shah Jahan, they were called *'the beast of prey...outwardly obedient servitors'*. Generally, there have been negative assessments of the tribesmen, yet the British, at heart, had respect for their spirit and skill.

Colonel H.D. Hutchison, who participated in the Tirah campaign, said *"...These men are extremely bold, they are as cunning and clever as they are audacious. They show much patience in watching and waiting for their prey, and great dash and impudence in their attacks when they make them."*

Understanding a Pathan

Therefore, at the outset, it would be wise to understand the intricate system of tribes whereby the different clans were independent in nature from each other, only to combine against common foe. Even their relationship with Afghanistan was only due to ethnic kinship, but independent of domination – either administrative or political. A tribe was further divided into kinship groups referred as *'khels'*. They never were under an organized control of any power, remained free and thus not taxed. They resisted any aligned move into their areas.

Of Pathans, there are some virtues expected – courage (*'tureh'*), taking revenge (*'badal'*), protecting honour (*'ghayrat'*). Eldest male member holds authority in an extended family. Fredrick Barth's anthropological study suggests that "feuding was avarice and the tribal code with its polarizing demands for *'melomastia'* (hospitality to strangers) and as *'nanavatai'* (sanctuary) to fugitives, preservation of personal *'nang'* (honour), *'badal'* (revenge against all enemies), was immutable. They follow the dictate of the tribal council (*'jirgah'*) to resolve conflicts and make decisions."

Their language *'Pashto'* is written in Perso-Arabic script. They are mostly of the Suni sect. They are largely communal, abiding unwritten code *'Pashtunwali'*, which makes them, stick together in the tribe. There were fights clan to clan, village to village and at times among themselves in the same village itself. They fought out till casualties swelled or ammunition finished. They settled issues by intermarriages. Men folk plundered, boasted of it and planned their next adventure or lazed. Women did the entire field and house cores. It was said that **'when you see an unhappy Pakhtoon, it means he is not fighting'**.

Geographical Allocation

The Tirah were divided in the main clans as follows:

* Maidan Valley was occupied by Zakka, Malikdin and Kamber Khel.
* Waran Valley by Zakkha and Akka.
* Rajgul Valley by Khuki Khel.
* South and Southeast of Bara, after Datoi were Kamar, Sipah and Zakka Khel.

The Afridis

They were considered to be the most avaricious of the races. They inhabit areas West of Peshawar, Khyber Pass and Maidan. They were the best fighters, apt in the use of weapons including saber, sword or rifle. They were certainly braver than most others and less treacherous. Hospitality was their virtue. They were of Sunni persuasions of the Mohammadan faith. They were influenced most by the Mullahs and Saiyids. Their contact with the outside world was through their religious heads. Their classification and number of fighters available were as follows:

* Khuki Khel – 4500.
* Malikdin Khel – 4000.
* Kambar Khel – 4500.
* Kamrai Khel – 600.
* Zakkha Khel – 4500.
* Sipah Khel – 1200.
* Aka Khel – 1800.
* Adam Khel – 5900.

The above totaled 27,000. The Adam Khel did not form part of the Afridis tribe as such. Their habits and interest were different from the others. The Zakkha Khel had the maximum area. They could easily move out in summers from East to West to cooler regions. Also, they could maneuver when under pressure. They were the toughest to fight with. They were richer because of the cultivable lands and abundance of money collected from subsidies lolled out by the British.

Their fighting qualities and tactics are summarized below:

* They had specialty in hill fighting.
* Almost all possessed a rifle of some sort or the other.
* They also possessed 1250 breach loading rifles they had stolen from the British.
* They employed spies to know the enemy and used this information to plan a raid.
* Knowledge of their plans was restricted to only chief raiders thus utmost surprise ensured.
* They spread false reports to mislead informers.

* They used darkness for success.
* Their skill at fire arms was remarkable since they employed ex-soldiers of native armies.
* They provoked desertion of native soldiers en-mass.

The Orakazais

They inhibit mountains North-West and North-East of Kohat, bounded on the North by the Afridis, on the South Miranzai and on the West Bangash country or Sufed Koh. They are offshoot of the Karlarni tribe of Pathans. They are connected with Afridis, Wazirs and Khattaks. Their original ancestry dates back to Wurak, a descendent of Kais, or Abdul Rashid, the Pathan. Their leaders of refute were Haji Khan, a ruthless orthodox man, Khan Masud, a wily fanatic, who played pawn in the hands of the Amir. There were seven clans that constitute the Orakazais (suffix of *'zai'* means family), these were:

* Ismailzai (Sunis) that had six sections, Rabia Khel, Akhel, Mamazai, Khadizai, Isa Khel and Sada Khel numbering 2000, lacking courage and badly armed.
* Massuzai (Sunis) – 5000 descendents of Masud most powerful. Their sections were Landaizai, Khawaja Khel and Alizai
* Lashkarzai (Sunis) – 6500. Their sections were Alisherza and Mamuzai. They had the maximum horses.
* Daulatzai – 2200 staunch fighters, fanatical, prosperous, better armed, fairly brave. Their sections comprised Firoz Khel, Bizoti and Utman Khel.
* Four sections of Muhammad Khel (Shias). – 2500. Their sections were Bar Muhammad, Abdul Aziz, Mani Khel and Sipaya. They were well armed, bravest of the Orakazai.
* Two sections of Sturi Khel/Alizai (mixes of Shias and Sunis) – 700 who were poorly armed. Their sections were Bara Sturi and Tirah.
* Hamsaya clans (Sunis) – 9800 courageous personnel. Their sections were Ali Khel, Mala Khel, Mishti and Sheikhan.

Orakazai fighters numbered 22,680 Sunnis and 5,730 Shias.

The defence system of the two tribes differed because of the geographical conditions of the areas held by them. Summarily, both had narrow, tortuous, precipitous defiles that had slippery boulders, steep slopes which were a nightmare to the British and tough going for the native troops, but were a cake walk for the tribesmen since born and brought up there. Only Gurkhas were a match, the Sikhs soon becoming accustomed. The difference lay because the Orakazai country side did not have natural shelters for refuge which was available in plenty to the Afridis in the North and towards the Afghan territories.

The Pathans were swayed by the words of Mullahs, of eminence Powind Mulla, the Miangul of Swat and the Fakir of Ipi, who were actually revered by the tribals. It would be quite in place to say that the root cause of the outbreak was the fanatics of the tribesmen, in whatever capacity it might be taken, and it was subject to influences.

However, in Afghan view and which cannot be denied, they fought for their freedom, to safeguard their territories, religion and homes. They called the **'forward policy'** of the British **'annexation by the infidel'**. The igniting argument was 'holy Swat practically annexed, a garrison established at Malakand, a permanent post at Chakdara', all this at the expense of the original proclamation of a short occupation that was promised. They believed there was erosion of their honour because of constant and deliberate actions by the British. Construction of roads and establishment of military posts were considered a threat to a slow and definite finish of the 'Pashtuns'.

Starting from the first expedition in 1850, the British launched seven against the Afridis and four against the Orakazais.

Another aspect that has to be understood is the relationship the Pashtoons had among themselves and as clan to clan. The system of hereditary blood feuds persisted, from father to son, generation to generation, though in many cases the original reason for the bad blood was not known. Similarly, there were fights and skirmishes among different clans, only to be forgotten for the duration of a fight against the common enemy. There were fights even within a village.

The British Policy

The British Government used varied tools to keep the tribesmen in check – bribing Chiefs, adopting policy of 'divide and rule', arresting one in place of the other wanted from a family, blatant exploitation of the illiterate oriental mind and destruction of their properties. The younger generation, in particular, took the tribute paid by the British Government to Khyber tribes as payment out of fear and not as a policy to look after them. The younger people had no employment. They naturally were drawn to the opportunity the situation offered to prove their worth and assuage their personal honour. They resorted to fighting and carried out raids and ambushes in defiance of their elders. They accepted challenge seeking to enhance their prestige and that of the clan they came from.

Afghan Turbulence and British Reactions

Important events of trouble in NWFP durning 1800-1897, are tabulated below:

- # 1800 – British envisaged NWFP to be vulnerable.
- # 1839 – Colonel Wade occupied Khyber.
- # 1838-42 – First Anglo-Afghan war.
- # 1850-97 – Seven expeditions launched against Afridis and four against Orakazais.
- # 1855 – Lt Col Craige defeated Aka Khel Afridis.
- # 1877-78 – Expeditions against Jawakis by Generals Keys and Ross.
- # 1878 – Expedition at Bazar Valley launched to check harassment by Afridis at lines of communication at Khyber Pass. 3500 troops quelled Zakha Khel Afridis. An agreement was signed with following main points:
  - * Independence of Afghanistan accepted but no interference from any other country.
  - * Afghanistan shall be responsible for law and order at Khyber Pass area.
  - * Permit system shall prevail for entrance to Khyber.
  - * A Subsidy of Rs 87,540 was levied on Afghanistan.
- # Jun 1878 – the Jawaki Area also agreed to the above conditions. However, minor expeditions continued to deal with irritants like raids and plunder by tribesmen. Many tribes failed to submit the fines levied, hence expeditions towards Miranzai were undertaken in 1855, 1869 and 1891. To protect the border at Miranzai, three posts were established at Gulistan, West of Sangar and Lakka. It was a psychological gain over the tribesmen. A corps of Khyber

Rifles was created and established at the new posts Ali Masjid, Landi Kotal and Maude under a British commandant. To counter this, there was an outbreak of hostilities on the incitement of Mullahs and Maliks. However, their call of *'Jihad'* was not favoured by the Amir. In July 1897, there was an attack on the escort of a political officer at Tochi. In July and August, they attacked in thousands at Malakand, Chakdara, Shankargarh, Shabkadar, Jamrud, Khyber, Bara, Fort Maude, Gulistan, Shinawari and Hangu Camp. Estimated about 2,00,000 Pathans were up in arms. Details:

July 1897 – Political officer and escorts attacked at Tochi.

26 July 1897 – Malakand and Chakdara posts attacked by 20,000 tribesmen. Looted arms, ammunition and other provisions.

31 July 1897 – Malakand siege lifted by Malakand Force.

02 August 1897 – Chakdara cleared.

07-09 August 1897 – Hadda Mullah burnt Shankargarh (an old Sikh cantonment bazar) and attacked Shabkadr post (fort built by the Sikhs) with 5,000 men.

15 August 1897 – Afridis moved towards Jamrud Fort.

21 August 1897 – Afridis attacked Khyber, Jamrud and Bara forts.

23 August 1897 – Khyber and Fort Maude relieved from tribesmen.

26 August 1897 – Samana and Gulistan fort threatened by a large force.

28 August 1897 – Shinwari post attacked and destroyed.

29 August 1897 – The Pathjans took action against Hangu.

The Kohat garrison was reinforced with 9 Field Battery RA, 18 Bengal Lancers and 15 Sikhs. During the months of August-September, the Pathans attacked the posts at Samana, this again was not supported by the Amir. The British resolved to react decisively and undertook the Tirah Campaign.

Treaties and Treacheries

It is true that Afridis had been incited and ignited by the religious zealots and these very overtures were indicative to other clans for raising their heads. But as discussed earlier this was not the only harbinger of overall rising that erupted at Chakdara and Malakand in a short time. There were other causes too.

The crux of the rationale for a campaign lay in the formulation of the treaties and the violations thereto which have already been analysed in the first chapter.

The main reasons for hatred of the tribesmen towards the British were:

- The tribesmen felt the British had gone back on clauses of the Treaty of 1891 and were consolidating their positions in NWFP.
- Religious fanaticism.
- Durand Line, dividing their lands.
- The British trying to spread Christianity and influencing their women folk who had taken refuge with them.
- The adventurist lore of the younger generation.

The Tirah Campaign

On 04 August 1897, Deputy Commissioner of Kohat conveyed to Peshawar that Mullah Sayed Akbar had been able to incite Orakazais for a rising. This information was not taken seriously. On 17 August, further information was received that a *'lashkar'* (an army) of ten thousand had assembled to capture posts of Khyber Rifles. Still, there was no response. The Afridis attacked the posts at Ali Masjid and Jamrud. As a reaction on 03 September 1897, it was decided to punish the Afridis.

It was more or less a religious crusade undertaken by the Pathans. A religious pamphlet by Amir was an igniting instrument. The sentences in the book had double meaning, conceived and written by a cunning mind. For example, one of the quotation was formed as, "The need of those persons who defend the frontier of Mohamedan territories for one prayer is equivalent to five hundred prayers of those who stay at home and do not proceed to the frontier for keeping watch."

On the 14 August 1897, orders were given for creating three reserve brigades under Brigadier Generals Sir Bindon Blood, Westmacott and AG Yeatman Biggs, at Parachinar, Peshawar and Kohat respectively. 225 rifles of 36th Sikhs (4 Sikh) were with Parachinar garrison and remaining at Hangu. Concentration of forces was against heavy odds of terrain, large opposition and difficulties of move of armaments and transport. The campaign lasted till 03 April 1898.

The degree of success of this large expedition is discussed later in Chapter Seven.

36th Sikhs defended the Samana Ridge from 02 January till 03 October, thereafter formed part of 4th Brigade of Tirah Expeditionary Force. It operated with elan throughout the campaign winning three Battle Honours.

Sum Up

This then were the Pathans or Pashtoons, martial to the hilt, masterly skilful in warfare evolved by experience. They were the settlers in Afghanistan and NWFP, having come from almost all regions of Asia. The feudal system taught them affinity among themselves, natural or necessitated. They had been in an unending conflict that was a binding attribute that surged into a mutual sense of honour, affection and reverence. They lived in clans, fought among them, individual to individual, clan to clan, race to race and any invader. The tough country, difficult livelihood, and challenges of all sort of vagaries taught them survival in adversity. Their pride in their religion and beliefs, legitimacy to home and hearth, unacceptability of outsiders, are to be admired, and history seen in an independent pragmatic perspective.

"Truth can be stated in thousand ways, yet each one can be true."

– Sawami Vivekananda

LOCATION OF TRIBES

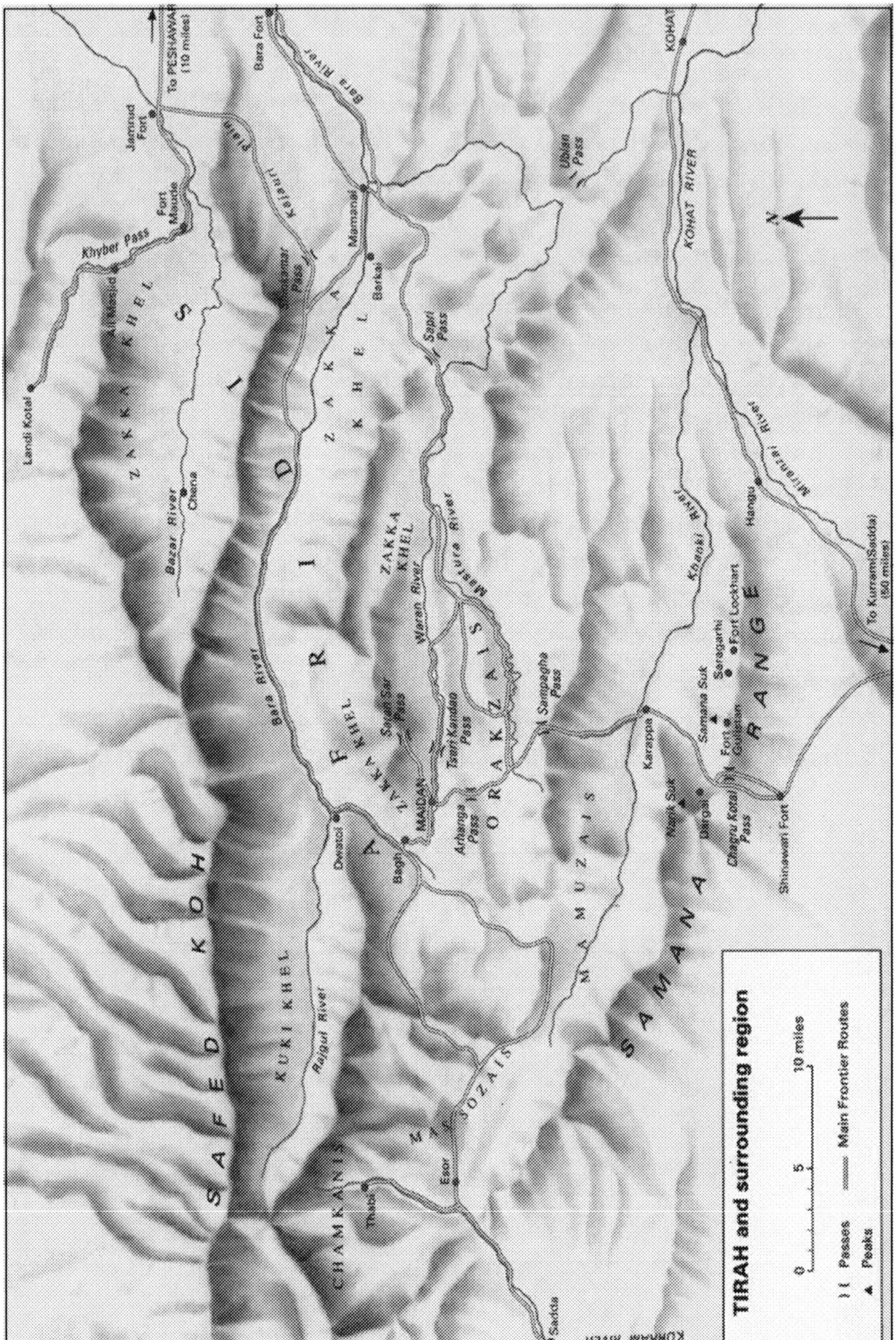

TRIBESMEN OF NWFP

"JIRGAH" IN PROGRESS

TRIBESMEN OF NWFP

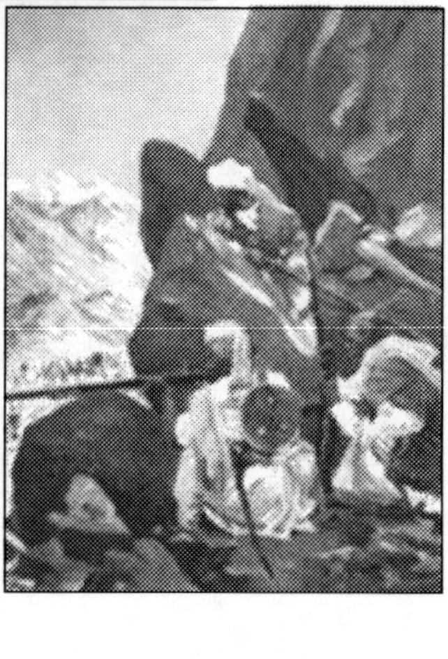

Positioned Behind Sangars

CHAPTER THREE

THE SIKHS

General

Numerous races from different regions and a diversity of soldiers of varying persona participated in the battles and campaigns in Afghanistan and the Frontier. They all proved their loyalty, dedication and valour – the Gurkhas and Punjabis – the Sikhs, the Hindus and the Muslims. The natives were the mainstay of the British Indian Army, besides of course the British and Irish themselves, who apart from providing leadership, fought like mercenaries adapting to local conditions like fish to water.

Those who fought at Saragarhi and at other posts on Samana in August-September 1897, were Sikhs, it would thus be of interest to know them better. It would be relevant to mention that four other Sikh units 14th Ferozepur Sikhs (later 1 Sikh, now 4 Mechanised), 15th Ludhiana Sikhs (now 2 Sikh), 35th Sikhs (now Sikh Regimental Center) and Ratray's Sikhs (now 3 Sikh), some Punjab, Patiala and Jind Forces, units and regiments, artillery, cavalry and logistics units had Sikhs on their roll. Therefore, it would be in the fitness of things to understand a race that did magnificent tasks joyfully, dedicatedly, displaying outright chivalry with spectacular achievements to their credit which were highly appreciated by their superiors and compatriots.

The Transformation and Beliefs

One of the most remarkable transformations in the chronicles of history is the unique evolvement of a pious peaceful people into a race of marvelous fighters who knew no fear. It is the development and grooming of the Sikhs which became a religious fraternity, then a military brotherhood, and from there to an organized power.

The Sikh religion was founded by Guru Nanak Dev who was born in 1469. It was a time when oppression of the weak was appallingly uncalled for. The perpetrators were not only from foreign lands but also natives. The society was divided on region, caste or religion lines. That was the time Guru Nanak propounded a philosophy that was much ahead of his time. He observed shortcomings of both Hindus and Muslims that had slowly ingrained into blind rituals. He preached love and understanding. He had nine successive Gurus, who during their time evolved far reaching considerations to live in society, pray to God Almighty, and be truthful to humanity.

The word 'Sikh' means disciple of God. The Sikhs believe in teachings of their ten Gurus whose sermons have been enshrined in the Guru Granth Sahib, their holy book, which is their Living Guru as ordained by the Tenth Guru. The Sikhs believe in 'One God' of all the people and religions, affirming monotheism. The Sikhs keep balance between spiritual as well as temporal obligations, exemplifying ultimate belief in God by living a virtuous life, and not be a celibtate or ascetic and denunciate the world as such. Sikhism preaches equality of people of any race, religion or sex.

God is one, formless, eternal and unobserved – an impersonal and transcendental creator. He is omnipresent and infinite. God has no gender. It is pernicious to live under the influences of ego, anger, greed, attachment and lust. The teachings do not profess final destination of heaven or hell, but on spiritual union with God resulting into knowledge and salvation.

Guru Nanak had sermonized when besides wrong practices among people; there was tyranny through merciless propagation by high and mighty placements, racial differences were galore and marauders prevailed through guile and force. Babar had established the Mughal Empire. Nanak propagated, *"There is no Hindu, there is no Muslim'*. To convey his message and to rinse the society of ills and evil that prevailed, he made long journeys to all the four cardinal directions and propagated his way of thinking with great effect. He chose Guru Angad Dev as his successor as he was more suited than his own sons. Angad continued the work and philosophy of Guru Nanak. He standardized the Gurmukhi script. The third Guru was Amar Das who established the city of Goindwal. He preached equality of gender, prohibited '*Pardah*' (women to cover their faces) and 'Sati' (sacrifice on the pyre of her husband). He encouraged '*langar*' (sit together and eat same food) for all. The fourth successor, Guru Ram Das established

Amritsar and got the Harmandir Sahib built there. The fifth Guru, Arjan Dev was responsible for compiling the Sikh scriptures, the Adi Granth. He was prosecuted by the Mughals who were suspicious of his religious fervour. This inspired his successor Guru Har Gobind Ji to a military and political organization. He created the '*Akal Takhat*' (Throne of the Timeless), a decision-making centre where '*Sarbat Khalsa*' (a representative get-together of *Khalsa*) is held to issue '*Gurmatas*' for all Sikhs to follow. He carried two swords, one for spiritual and the other temporal reasons (*Miri* and *Piri*). He organized and trained a force to defend them.

In 1644, Guru Har Rai, took over, and besides his religious responsibilities, provided medicines and succor to the needy and treatment to all. The eighth Master was Guru Har Krishan, he eradicated disease and famine and saved the people of Delhi by sacrificing his own life. The ninth guru, Teg Bahadur, sacrificed himself to save the Kashmiri Pandits from forcefully conversion to Islam. He was executed by Aurangzeb. That became the last nail in the coffin of the kingdom of the Mughals.

'*Ghalugharas*' (Holocast or Massacre)

The first '*ghalughara*' happened during the Afghan Provincial Government's campaign to wipe out the Sikhs during Mughal reign. It continued for years after the martyrdom of Guru Arjan Dev.

The Second '*Vada Ghalughara*' (the Great Massacre) occurred in 1762, near Malerkotla (Punjab). During his sixth invasion, Ahmed Shah Abdali decided to destroy the Sikhs totally. In his effort, he killed more than 30,000 Sikhs, almost 70% of the race lost their lives. The destruction of the Sikhs for ever became an irritant in the psyche of the race to avenge the killings by the Afghans.

Rise of 'Khalsa'

The tenth Guru was Gobind Rai, who took to Guruship at a tender age of nine years. He militarized his followers, created the 'Khalsa' in 1669. He asked a congregation for a head to be sacrificed. Five disciples volunteered one by one, as were asked each time by the Guru. The explicit wonder and coincidental that they all were from all types of strata, caste and hailed from different states, a shopkeeper from Lahore (Punjab), one from Meerut (UP), a calico printer from Dwarka (Gujrat), a water bearer from Jagannath

Puri (Orissa) and a barber from Bidr (Karnatka). All were baptized as *'Panj Piyaras'* (the five beloved ones), a collective name. The authority to decide Sikh affairs was placed on them. He got himself baptized by the *'Panj Piyaras'*. The Sikh community now was significantly transferred into a race of 'Saint-Soldiers' who developed their own political identity. He sacrificed his own four sons fighting the Mughals. He himself died in the process of fighting, but not before he had formed a race that provided the best of soldiers – bravest of the brave – an unprecedented shield of superb human beliefs, valour and sacrifice. He was a great poet who composed hymns in – Punjabi, Bhojpuri, Sanskrit and Pharisee – that resonate with his super wealth of knowledge, practical forebodings and martial inspiration. He compiled the *'Dasam Granth'*.

Guru Gobind Singh also gave a distinct identity to the Sikhs who were to have *'Amrit'* prepared by the *'Panj Piaras'*, to the tune of *'Shabad'* (*Gurbani*). The Sikhs were to add *'Singh'* (Lion) after their name and woman *'Kaur'* (Princess). They were to wear five 'Ks' – *'Kes'* (hair), *'Kara'* (steel bangle), *'Kanga'* (hair comb), *'Kirpan'* (sword) and *'Kachha'* (underwear). The *'Khalsa'* was to adhere to all the tenants of Sikh religion. They were to fight to defend the righteousness and the oppressed against totalitarianism.

> *"Oh ye men, whosoever desires to play in love of God, come to me with thy head on your palm"*.
>
> – Guru Gobind Singh

(To quote Robert F Kennedy: *"It is from numberless diverse acts of courage and belief that human history is shaped. Each time a man stands for an ideal, or acts to improve the lot of others, or strikes out against injustice, he sends forth a tiny ripple of hope, and crossing each other from a different center of energy and daring, those ripples build a current that can sweep down the mightiest walls of suppression and resistance"*.)

When breathing his last in 1703 AD, the Guru ordained that thereafter the 'Guru Granth Sahib', the holy book, shall be the 'Living Guru', a spiritual successor. Thus all the spiritual guidance required for their day to day life shall be from the 'Guru Granth Sahib', the eternal Guru, which also contained the writings of other faiths, whose messages were in keeping with the sermons of the Gurus. 'Sikhism' does not have priests; it has *'Garanthis'* (custodians).

The Sikh community soon became a regional force. It, however, must be understood that Guru Gobind Singh never proclaimed himself to be a King or General and thus any comparison with those who were so is an argument of the absurd. He was a saint-soldier, a *'marad agamra'* (man par excellence – man of unparallel virtues), who, because of the prevalent circumstances, raised soldiers to fight the tyranny and yet were pious. He laid emphasis on building up a strong base in Punjab rather than to move against the Mughal Empire; thereby utilizing the services of Pathans. He defended faith and not the territories.

Before his journey to eternal abode, the Guru appointed Lachhman Das, an ascetic, to be in charge of the Khalsa. He was baptised and named as Gurbakhash Singh but popularly came to be called Banda Singh Bahadur. He led the Sikhs from the front against the Mughal Empire and won many a battle, marching hundreds of miles, punishing the perpetrators of cruelty and unfair means. He was the first to establish the roots of the Sikh empire. He was, however, ultimately captured and mercilessly executed by the Mughals at Sirhind in 1716. The Sikhs, thereafter, for thirty years were rudderless and scattered, often resorting to acts of outlaws.

Meanwhile, the Mughals had weakened; voids were filled by local armies the gallant Marathas under Shiva Ji Maharaj, Scindias, Rorkelas and Gaikwads. The chivalrous Rajputs organized kingdoms in Rajasthan under Rajput Kings. The Jats raised their armies around Delhi. The Sikhs in Punjab, formed twelve *'Misals'* a sort of loose confederations who had intrigues among themselves, often resorting to battles. They combined superficially only against the foreign invaders. It was a commonwealth, military in character based on religion. They played havoc with the armies of Ahmed Shah Abdali on their return through Punjab after loot in the interiors of India. They snatched back the booty and liberated the Indian women from the clutches of invaders and restored them to their families. They used guerilla tactics, were fabulous riders, marvelous fighters, fearless, maintaining their faith and customs. Abdali had this to say, *"one day they will rule."*

Maharaja Ranjit Singh (1780-1839)

Then rose Maharaja Ranjit Singh, son of Sardar Mahan Singh, of Shukarchakia *'misal'* from Gujranwala, (now in Pakistan), who with his masterful mixture of diplomacy and force welded all the *'misals'* into a magnificent kingdom, that extended over Punjab, in the South-East up to the River Sutlej and in the North-West across the Indus. He had raised an efficient army of 70,000, duly trained by the British, the French and the Russians instructors. His army included the Sikhs, Punjabi Musalmans, Dogras and Gurkhas. He selected the best of Generals – Hari Singh Nalwa, Mohkam Chand, Akali Phoola Singh, Sham Singh Atariwala, Zorawar Singh, Jean Baptista Ventura (trained infantry), Jean Francois Allard (trained cavalry), Van Contlandt, Italian Paolo de Avitable, Spaniard Senor Oms, American Josiah Harlan (doctor, statesmen, soldier and scholar) Misr Dewan Chand, Mian Singh, Bal Bahadur, Lehna Singh Majithia (brains behind ordinances), Ghause Khan and Sheikh Elahi Baksh. His own sons Sher Singh, Kharak Singh and grandson Naunihal Singh were great warriors.

Ranjit Singh was an outstanding soldier, was conspicuous for his utmost vigour, shrewdness in judgment and promptness in action. He had great visions yet practical in immediate measure. He had made up his mind not to cross swords with the British and thus resorted to advances towards North and the Northwest.

The Maharaja was ever eager to break into new lands. Once he steadied himself in Punjab, his attention was cast towards Afghanistan where turmoil was the order of the day and weak Shah Shujah failed in his attempts to assume kingship. The Maharaja, also craved for the alluring valley of Kashmir, ultimately defeated the Afghans who were in possession for some decades. He had also set his eyes on the valleys of Kandhar and around. In 1818, the Sikhs captured Multan. He made an attempt towards Kandhar, which more or less was to have a feel of it. He captured Dera Ismail Khan and Ghazi Khan in 1822. The very next year he fought a well matched battle at Nowshera, he was victorious and added Peshawar to his suzerainty. He placed a Barakazai Chief as the Governor who paid annual tributes to him.

Shah Shuja, once again, tried in 1832, for the throne, and approached the Maharaja for support. In return, he accepted Ranjit Singh's demand of all areas which came to be known later as NWFP. He also presented the priceless diamond, Koh-I-Noor to the Maharaja. Yet his own efforts to capture the throne failed.

Ranjit Singh fought gruesome battles in the Frontiers. His forces under his gallant sons Princes Sher Singh and Kharak Singh and eminent generals Hari Singh Nalwa and Phula Singh defeated the Ghazis (Orakazais). The cries of *'Jihad'* were raised many times to finish the infidels. The enthusiastic Afghans were inflamed, decided to do or die for the 'green banner'. The Afridis, Yousafsais and Khattaks gathered as locust swarms. Thousands joined Mohammed Azim Khan's march from Kabul to Peshawar. It was quite a precarious situation at one time when Maharaja himself moved hastily to reinforce the beleaguered Sikh forces. The situation was reversed. The Afghans lost to better trained, well armed, led sterlingly, disciplined and motivated Khalsa Army. The battle at Naoshera was their death-knell. The Maharaja entered Peshawar to a roaring welcome. He made it a tributary to the Sikh empire, Yar Mohammed, a Barakazai having been appointed as Governor.

In 1823, Mohammed's half brother, in insolence to the Maharaja marched from Kabul with a large force. General Hari Singh Nalwa, along with Dewan Kirpa Ram and Prince Sher Singh crossed the Indus towards Attock. Meanwhile, the Maharaja along with Akali Phoola Singh and the renowned Gurkha Commander Bal Bahadur crossed the river near Jehangira. The Afghans were outclassed and totally demoralized. They tried to give battles but were defeated.

Yet in 1827, Sayyid Ahmed redeemed the Yousafzais who fought with the Sikhs under Budh Singh Sandhawalia. The Pathans fought a magnificent battle, but were crushed decisively; 8000 Sikhs defeating 1,50,000 Mohamadens.

Hari Singh Nalwa was made Governor of Pehawar in 1837. He conquered Jamrud. This gave an opportunity to the Sikhs to enter the Khyber Valley. Dost Mohammad Khan was now worried about the approach that lay open to Jalalabad, and thence to Kabul. But to his good luck, Maharaja Ranjit Singh had withdrawn maximum possible forces to Amritsar for celebrations of the marriage of his grandson Naunihal Singh. Aim was also to demonstrate his prowess to the British Commander-in-Chief who had been invited. Dost Mohammad took advantage of the situation and sent a substantial force against Shabqadar, Jamrud and Peshawar. Hari Singh Nalwa was prepared for an engagement. However, both sides had been instructed by their Supremes to exercise restraint. Yet the Afghans surrounded the small fort of Jamrud. Hari Singh Nalwa led his forces from Peshawar and advanced to Jamrud. Though the Sikhs were in small number, the thousands of Afghans panicked and scattered. While entering the fort, Hari Singh Nalwa was wounded mortally. He ordered his men not to divulge the news till reinforcements arrived. Though Jamrud was saved but this was also the end for the Sikhs for any further adventures towards the Afghan territories.

This then was the legacy left by the formidable Sikh forces for the British at the time of annexation of Punjab by the latter, after fighting some splendid battles which left both sides in awe and appreciation of each other. The testament to this appreciation by the British was inclusion of the Sikhs in the British Army. It was the recognition of the bravery, honesty, integrity and fearlessness of the Sikh soldier which impressed the British.

Annexation of Punjab by the British

It hardly took ten years after the demise of Maharaja Ranjit Singh for the great Raj to start crumbling due to dissentions. This also was the beginning of the Anglo-Sikh wars. Three prominent battles were fought during the First Anglo-Sikh War. In Battle of Mudki in December 1845, the Sikhs gave an excellent account of their fighting qualities. The famous historian Cunningham noted, "*...The resistance met was wholly unexpected.... Darkness and the obstinacy of the contest threw the English into confusion...the Colonels knew not what had become of their regiments they commanded, or the army of which they formed a part.*" The Sikhs had won the day but for treachery of some ranks. Reinforcements to the British led them to another fiercet battle at Ferozeshah on 21-22 December 12 miles from Mudki. The battle ensued throughout the night, '*fate of the British India trembled in the balance...*'. The British were on the verge of defeat and the Generals conferred to submit '*unconditional surrender*'. But fate dictated something else. For reasons unknown, the Sikhs withdrew the next day to Aliwal. They then moved to Sabraon by 10 February to fight another gallant battle. There was treason among the Sikhs, by Tej Singh and Gulab Singh Dogra. Tej Singh with his armies fled, and while crossing the Sutlej, destroyed the boats. Lord Gough had this to say, '*Policy, however precluded me publicaly by recording sentiments on the splendid gallantry of our fallen foe, or to record acts of heroism displayed not only by the Sikh Sirdars and army; and I declare, were if not from a deep conviction that my country's good required the sacrifice, I would have wept to have witnessed the fearful slaughter of so devoted a body of men.*' Lord Hardinge said, "*Few escaped, none it may be said, surrendered. The Sikhs met their fate with the resignation which distinguishes their race.*" The British suffered unparalleled casualties in these battles.

The British moved their forces into Lahore. The Sikh Army was disbanded. The districts of Jallundhur, Hoshiarpur and Kangra were transferred to the British. The Kashmir valley was sold to Raja Gulab Singh for a paltry sum. The minor, Dalip Singh, son of Maharaja Ranjit Singh, was installed as a puppet king of the remaining areas. The soldiers of the disbanded units realized the deceit and felt enraged. They united under their patriotic Sardars and fought the Second Anglo-Sikh War at Chillianwala on 13 January 1849. The place had reminiscence of earlier battles between Alexander and Porus in 1600 B.C. Generals Sham Singh and Jawahar Singh Nalwa were the Sikh leaders. Both sides suffered heavy casualties. The British were again on the verge of a defeat when it rained for three days and the British were rescued. They were able to withdraw. By the time the last battle at Gujrat was fought, the British were able to get reinforcements. Both sides fought bravely, the battle results were ding dong in one hand and the other. Ultimately, the Sikhs lost ground, fighting with valour and sacrifice. It was 14 March 1849 when the British won the day ultimately. Punjab was annexed.

Acceptance of Sikh Valour by the British

The British were quick to appreciate the need to form regiments of the Punjabis, especially of the Sikhs. The Regiment of the Ferozepur Sikhs (1 Sikh, now 4 Mech) and the Regiment of Ludhiana Sikhs (now 2 Sikh) were raised for service with the Bengal Army as per General Orders issued at Shimla on 30 July 1846. The men belonged to Majha and Malwa areas that were under the British protection during the reign of Maharaja Ranjit Singh and subsequent heirs. XIV Ferozepur Sikh was raised on 30 July 1846 and XV Ludhiana Sikh on 01 August 1846. It was followed by raising XLV Rattary's Sikh in 1856, the composition being that of Sikhs, Punjabi Musalmans and Dogras. By 1885, the unit was converted to pure Sikhs. All the three battalions fought in a number of operations in India as well as outside the country, winning commendable laurels.

Additional raising of 35th (XXXV, now Sikh Regimental Center), at Ferozepur on 29th April 1887 and 36th (XXXVI, now 4 Sikh) on 23rd March 1887 at Jallundur, were undertaken for Bengal Infantry, besides some other battalions and cavalry squadrons. The Sikh battalions participated in battles and campaigns in NWFP, winning gorgeous accolades for their glorious achievements, steadfastness, valour and sacrifice.

There were some irregular forces during the Sikh reign who were employed to safeguard the 'Raj' interest in the Frontiers. Out of them and numerous other 'soldiers of fortune', the British raised the Punjab Irregular Frontier Force or "PIFFERS" of Punjabis and Gurkhas.

There, of course, were numerous units and regiments which had Punjabis in their ranks, but since this book is more to emphasize the soldiers who fought at Saragarhi, the additional stress laid on the Sikh units obviously is more prominent.

The roots of valourous legacy, seeded through selfless service as the sword arm to the destitute, beginning with the Sikh Gurus, several 'misals', unflinching service to a Government. The outstanding deeds are written in golden letters, might it be 1947-48, 1962, 1965, 1971 or 1999, missions overseas or numerous insurgencies that have erupted from time to time. They are there, shoulder to shoulder – chivalrous, patriotic, sacrificing and living to their glorious record.

General Sir Charles Gough has this to say: *"The Sikh nation itself is interesting. Its evolution was marked by characteristics unique among Oriental states, while the race thereby developed forms one of the finest fighting type to be found, whether in Asia or Europe; bearing, indeed, a distinct resemblance in some particulars to the democratic soldiery of the Parliament and the Covenant"*.

"The Hero, entering the field,
Fights on without quailing.
Know that man to be true hero,
Who fights in defence of the defenceless,
Hacked limb by limb,
He still flees not the field."

– Bhagat Kabir

Guru Nanak Dev
Founder of Sikhism

Guru Gobind Singh
Founder of Khalsa (warriors)

Ten Gurus

Guru Granth Sahib
Essence of Teachings of Gurus and Saints

Banda Singh Bahadur

Maharaja Ranjit Singh

Maharaja Sher Singh

General Hari Singh Nalwa

CHAPTER FOUR

THE BRITISH

General

The British had inherited a legacy left over by the Khalsa Empire in NWFP, which had become a cockpit of international rivalry and tension. The main parties were Russia, Iran, Afghanistan, British India and England. Each action by an adversary caused complications for the British.

Situational Developments

If the original frontier with Russia is considered it was almost a thousand miles away, but as the lines of influences advanced, the distance from the Kazakh Steppes to the NWFP with Afghanistan, reduced drastically hence the threat became more realistic to British India. In keeping up with the Crimean War of 1854-6, British also stepped up their advances in Central Asia. Here, they had to deal with prosperous Uzbeks in Afghan Turkistan, across the River Oxus. Then there were the Tajiks around Herat and Kabul. The Afghans were a mix of locals and settlers. They lived around Herat and Seistan. They also included Pathans of NWFP. Ahmed Shah Abdali, a Durrani, tried to weld Afghanistan together. Nadir Shah of Persia in 1737 who earlier held sway over Afghanistan, NWFP and torched Delhi, left behind Ahmed Shah Abdali to rule. Nadir Shah's son Timur Shah ruled for two decades, leaving the reins to his son, Shah Zaman, who proved to be weak. This encouraged the British to launch the First Afghan War in 1838-42. The British supported Painda Khan, a Durrani, who plotted against Zaman Shah and placed his brother Shah Shuja, on the throne. The tussle continued among the different clans, the advantage going to Maharaja Ranjit Singh and subsequently to the British.

The Britons

As history goes, for over 10,000 years, Britain an island, had been invaded by numerous adventurers, the new ones either displacing earlier settlers or becoming a part of the fascinating ethnic sphere established, though there had always been a basic continuity of population. The island was more or less a geographical entity and had no political meaning and no single identity but was mostly under the sway of the Romans around 52 AD. An identity was only created in 1707 with the union of England, Wales and Scotland, affected by James I of England and VI of Scotland.

Numerous cultural groups in England having identity across the seas, looked back for a natural connect. Because of its contiguous geographical and group similarities, Ireland was seen as a part of Britain. There had been a regional diversity of culture that survived a few generations to split or merge. There were thus natural conflicts for survival, for the lure of more. They mostly spoke English, classified as a Germanic tongue. The invasions by Romans started AD 43, but they did not colonize the islands to any significant degree, Scotland not been captured. The invading 'barbarians' Anglo-Saxons, moved Westwards to overwhelm the Romans, that resulted into the development of new small kingdoms, in the Welsh and Cornish regions.

The long history thus suggests absorption of a multitude of people with an indigenous population, who formed the majority. From original 'Celtic' uniformity, it changed hands to Romans, Saxons and other invaders and thus Britain is home to multiple peoples. This is the country of adventurous brave races that combined to form a most formidable empire, which always had an eye on other lands for trade or subjugation.

The Advent of the British to India

The rise of the British in India is a long story of initiatives, indulgences, maneuvers, brow-beating, connivances, skirmishes, and treaties. Promises made were honoured where advantageous, otherwise ignored unless opposed. A policy of *'divide and rule'* and purchasing the loyalties was the call of the day. Full advantage was taken of indigenous rivalries.

In 1740s, there was no European power in India. There were four trading companies vying with each other – Portuguese, Dutch, French and British.

The British were rebuffed by the Dutch and had lost in the East Asian Spice trade to Portugal. So they turned their efforts towards the Indian coast. In 1799, a group of merchants, in pursuance of *'quiet trade'* set out for green pastures in India. In due course of time, they formed the British East India Company (BEIC) and established trading posts in Surat (1619), Madras (1639), Bombay (1668) and Calcutta (1690). The Company rose to dominate almost half of the world's trade. It was also the beginnings of the British Empire in India. The initial focus of trade changed to hold territories.

Indian Turmoil: British East India Company (BEIC)

The BEIC acquired Madras (Chennai) from the Raja of Chandragiri in 1639. During the same period, Shah Jahan, the Mughal King consolidated his kingdom towards Golkunda and Karnatka. After an intriguing period in the Mughal ruling class, Aurangzeb took over the reins. He enforced an orthodox version of Islam, causing the Marhattas, Rajputs, Jats and Sikhs to rise against him in their respective regions Maharashtra, Rajasthan, Uttar Pradesh and Punjab respectively. By this time, the BEIC conquered Bombay (Mumbai) from Portugal in 1668. While the Mughals were fully engaged in their own fights to retain supremacy, the British won Calcutta (Kolkatta) in 1690. Guru Gobind Singh who had created an armed wing of the Sikhs was assassinated in 1708 AD. His chosen leader Banda Bahadur played havoc with the Mughal armies, but was ultimately defeated and executed in 1716. In 1736, at the end of the Nayak dynasty in South India, Madurai was purchased by the British. The Mughal hold in India started dwindling during the reign of Aurangzeb. There was eruption of turmoil and the British were forced to defend their trading posts against local rulers. They also had to contend with France, who had made significant ingress.

The traders suffered enormous losses. This then made the Government of Britain step in to take over. The traders did venture into conquests of areas which gradually were required to be administered by Governors, Viceroys and Commanders-in-Chief. Winning over of India, the 'crown jewel of the British Empire' influenced western civilization as much as it did South East Asia, in the fields of religion, social fiber, economy, politics, philosophy and history.

Change Over to Arms

The French recruited the locals as sepoys to fight their battles. The British followed suit. They defeated the French in the Battle of Arcot (Ascot), thus becoming a leading colonial power. There ensued a seven year war (1756-63) between the two, initially the French General Joseph Francois Duplex gaining some ground, ultimately the British General Robert Clive defeated the French at the Battle of Plassey. The British used all types of ruses to exploit. The local *'nawabs'* were won over by enticements of money and gifts. The British Government also lured their own people for service by offering lucrative emoluments and status. As a result, hundreds of Britishers applied for the jobs in India. Most did not like the tropical conditions of India but sustained it for the prospect of fortune. Many Britishers learnt the Indian languages and adapted to local conditions. Yet some claimed their superiority to the Indians thus alienating them, widening the gap and fostered discontent that grew by the day. In 1800, there was unrest due to the British Christian missionaries whose efforts clashed with the Hindus. Also, their fast system of trade and development was an eye-sore to the slow-paced Indians. The Great Mutiny of 1857 shook the British, though they held sway decades thereafter. Queen Victoria reduced BEIC, and British Crown assumed direct control of the Indian continent.

While Ahmed Shah Abdali, on his sixth invasion in 1761, at the Battle of Panipat, defeated the Marathas, starting the decline of their empire, the British expanded their influence towards Bihar. But in another direction they were defeated by Tipu Sultan who was the ruler of Mysore. They defeated Nawab Siraj-ud-Daula, Nawab of Bengal, Bihar and part of Odisa at Plassey in 1751 and was placed by Meer Jaffer.

In 1778, the Company had 67,300 Indian soldiers. It became an instrument of geo-political power and expansion. For better management, it had three Presidencies – Bengal, Madras and Bombay; each having its own arms and services. The three Pesidencies had a fighting strength of 2,80,000 by 1857 when the Indian Mutny took place. A number of 'Acts' were enacted by the Government to take over the affairs of the Company. The Rebellion of 1857 created devastation in India. In the aftermath, under the provisions of the Government in 1858, the British Government nationalized the Company, taking over its administrative powers and machinery, as well as its armed forces.

The British continued their advances and conquered Travancore in 1795. They then killed Tipu Sultan of Mysore in 1799. The British and the Marathas had most of India divided between them. The British also employed Indian troops abroad, in Sumatra and then in Egypt in 1800. The British fought two wars against the Marathas, 1775-82 and 1803-05; in the latter they defeated the Marathas. In 1805, they also concluded the Treaty of Amritsar with the Sikhs, which restricted both sides not to venture into each other's territories. The defeat of the Marathas made the British powerful rulers. They also captured Ceylon (Sri Lanka). The following year, Nepal became a British Protectorate after the Anglo-Nepal wars.

Interestingly, when the Sikhs captured Peshawar in 1834, the British invaded Afghanistan to expel the Iranians from Herat. The British had lost face in the First Anglo-Afghan War 1839-42, and returned to India in 1842. On the death of Maharaja Ranjit Singh, they fought the Anglo-Sikh Wars, Mudkee 18-21 December 1846, Ferozeshah 21-22 December 1846, Budhowal-Aliwal 23 December 1846-28 January 1847, Sobraon 10 February 1847; Multan July 1848 to January 1849 (two sieges); Chillianwala 4 Decmber-13 January 1849; and Gujarat 21 February 1849 where finally the Khalsa army was defeated concluding annexation of Punjab.

Consolidation

The credit for the institution of the British Indian Army and the raising of its first military units of the East India Company in Madras in 1748 goes to Major Stringer Lawrance, the father of the Indian Army. He was the first to be appointed Commander-in-Chief (C-in-C) of all the Company's forces. He organized them into three 'Presidencies'. He amalgamated the European and Indian troops, and Royal British Regulars. The 'Great Famine' in 1783, caused the people to die in great numbers. The alternative to agriculture was seen in the army – a blessing in disguise – providing salary, uniform and prestige. The army was transformed into an efficient force through intensive training and discipline. A system of secure pay and pension was started. In 1849, Lord Curzon, the Viceroy, instituted the Sindh Frontier Force (SFF) and the Punjab Frontier Force (PFF). The SFF, as part of army, was tasked to control the Balauch tribesmen and PFF deployed on the NW borders. The 5 Gurkha Regiment was also added to the PFF. Till 1866, PFF known as PIFFERS (Punjab Irregular Field Force), was under the control of the Lieutenant Governor of Punjab, then later under the C-in-C.

After the Indian Mutiny of 1857, India became a British Crown Colony. More British regiments were moved to India. The ratio of the British to Indians was increased from 1:10 to 1:3. A mix of units in a formation or a garrison was resorted to. Except for mountain gun batteries, other artillery units were placed under control of the Royal Artillery. In 1895, three armies of the Presidencies of Bombay, Madras and Bengal were incorporated into a single army. The senior officers especially, and most others were Britishers.

The Indian states provided troops to the British Indian Army, officered mostly by the Britishers for campaigns on the frontiers.

After annexation of Punjab on 29 January 1849, the Frontiers became difficult to control. For fifty years, after many expeditions, some control was established. The Second Anglo-Afghan War 1878-80, though successful militarily, was a misadventure. It lead to the Durand Line. This increased the area of responsibility. The high tough mountains were difficult to cross; the tribes were of an independent nature accepting no law, authority or rule. The superb ingenuity of the British came into play here when they pursued the old tact to recruit locals to protect their interests, however, under the overall management of the British. A number of agencies were established viz; Khyber, Kurram, Malakand and Waziristan.

Lord Curzon, the Viceroy, and Governor General instituted the PIFFERS.

This thus is the story of extreme opportunism, subterfuge, erosion of morals, treachery that embarked the British on a ruthless mission of expansion that had no bounds as long as success was gained, notwithstanding the means used in the garb of better rule and administration.

Organization of Indian Army

The principle for organization followed was not to allow any single class or caste to dominate or command another class or clan. Thus three different systems were adopted:

- The General Mixed System – each company in a regiment consisted of different races and castes which were mixed together irrespective of caste and creed.

- The Class Company System – each company in a regiment had soldiers of one caste and social clan. In this way each company was pure; different castes and classes were kept separately at the company level.
- The One Class Regiment System – men from one distinct social caste or class. At times, exclusion from one district/region.

The British Overbearing Precursors and Tribal Retaliation

The East India Company was dissolved in August 1858 and power was transferred to the British Government, who appointed Viceroys to oversee and govern. In 1876, Queen Victoria proclaimed herself as the Empress of India. In 1878, the British invaded Afghanistan to repel Russian expansionism. Afghanistan ceded Baluchistan to the British. In 1893, Afghanistan and British India agreed on a border splitting the Pashtun territories. The seemingly peace prevailed only for sixteen years, the Durand Line being the main bone of contention. The British continued to consolidate their position in NWFP to the chagrin of the Pathans. The latter were inspired by a religious fury, united in their resolve to overthrow the infidels once and for all. This created a precarious situation for the British. In 1897, the British were left with no alternative but to launch a massive campaign. They undertook the Tirah Expedition to take control of the Frontier.

Long innings in which the British were drawn from a business enterprise to colonization is a period of intrigues in which several countries were involved with complications for the British Indian Army. The effort has been to sum up almost four centuries of tussle for supremacy which adds richly to the character of the people involved – especially the Pathans, the Sikhs, the Indian soldiery, and the British.

The Indians of different regions and castes fought under the British with other natives viz; Bengalis against Punjabis and Marhattas, the Sikhs against the Biharis and Afghans. Basically, in essence they were mercinaries who for pay, perks and laurels fought under a foreign power against their own Indian brothern, also a legacy of internal rivalries and prejudices.

Queen Victoria

Robert Clive

England

CHAPTER FIVE

36 SIKHS (XXXVI): 4 SIKH

The Raising

The Battalion was initially raised as a Bareilly Levy in 1858. In May 1861, the Unit was redesigned as 40th Bareilly Regiment of Bengal Infantry. In 1861, it was renumbered as the 36th Regiment, Bengal Infantry. It is from this date that the Battalion takes its precedence in the Indian Army. The class composition at that time is not known. In 1864, a new scheme of mixed class composition of Bengal Infantry Regiments was introduced. The Battalion consisted of eight companies, two of Brahamins and Rajputs, one of Jats, two each of Ahirs and Kurmis and one company comprised of all races and castes.

In 1876, vide G.O. No. 60, Colours was granted to the Battalion.

In 1882, after a service of 24 years, as a part of overall scheme, it was reduced.

Re-raising

The Unit was re-raised at Jalandhar Cantonment vide Special Army Circular dated 23 March 1887 Clause 46 and GOC of 20 April 1887. The first Commanding Officer (CO) was Lieutenant Colonel James Cook. The Battalion was redesignated as 36 (Sikh) Regiment, Bengal Infantry. It comprised of eight wings of Jat Sikhs, from the Majha, Malwa and Doaba districts of Punjab. 225 all ranks (01 Subedar, 09 Jemadars, 25 Havildars, 26 Naiks and 164 Sepoys) from twenty regiments of Bengal Infantry and Frontier Force formed the initial part of the battalion. (Havildar Ishar Singh was from this group, transferred from 14 Sikhs that provided one Subedar, one Jemadar, five Havildars, four Naiks and 44 sepoys; what rank was Ishar Singh at that time is not known. He was a Havildar in 1987 and held the same rank for almost ten years). Between 01 May 1987 and 01 January 1888, vigorous recruitment was carried out under Lieutenant Colonel James Cook, Major TG Thomas, Captain HRL Holmes, Captain JF Woolridge, Lieutenants W.D. Gordon, C.E. Johnson and C.E.H. Erskine at Amritsar, Ferozepur, Gurdaspur, Jalandar, Lahore, Ludhiana, Nabha and Patiala. A total of 685 sepoys were recruited in the second lot which constituted 462 from South of the River Sutlej and 223 trans Sutlej. The maximum 177 were from Ludhiana while there were 152 from Patiala. The Regiment was brought to a strength of 912.

All the men were more than five feet eight inches tall and of 36 inches chest. Captain Holmes, who was a wrestler, would challenge the villagers at a wrestling bout and those who won were recruited, such was the standard ensured. He retired in 1892.

The recruitment age was between 17 and 20 years. Therefore, it can be concluded that keeping in mind the ten years gap till the Battle of Saragarhi, the average age would have been between 25 to 30 years, barring one or two who came in the first group and would have been older, or those few recruited during the ten years period to make up for retirements, discharges or casualties that would have occurred and would have thus been younger. This conclusion is amply clear from their roll numbers. This can also be substantiated from the fact that out of the 21 Saragarhi martyrs only four were married.

Dress

The dress of the soldiers was red turbans with yellow facings (*'safa'*). A quiot was worn on the turban. The men wore a red tunic broad *'patti'* in front. Ranks up to Havildar were in yellow stripes. The badge on the turban was engraved with 'XXXVI Sikhs' between two quoits, crown on top and surrounded by an embroidered border.

Officers

On 9th June 1887, the Battalion comprised of the following officers:-

(a) *Commandant,* Lieutenant Colonel J Cook (earlier Second-in Command 14th Sikhs).

(b) *Wing Commanders.*

(i) Major T G Thomas (Officiating Second-in Command 25 Punjab Infantry to be Second-in Command).

(ii) Captain H R L Holmes (Wing Officer 45th Ratray's Sikhs (3 Sikh) to be Wing Commander).

(c) *Wing Officers.*

(i) Captain J F Woolridge (Wing Officer 7th Bengal Infantry).

(ii) Lieutenant W D Gordon (Officiating Wing Officer 3 Sikh to be Wing Officer and Quarter Master).

(iii) Lieutenant H E Custance (Wing Officer 2nd Battalion 2nd Gurkhas on secondment to Burma Police).

(iv) Lieutenant C E Johnson (Wing Officer 27th Punjab Infantry to be Wing Officer and Adjutant).

(v) Lieutenant C T A Searle (On supernumerary strength)

(vi) Lieutenant C E H Erskine (On supernumerary strength of 11th Bengal Infantry to be Wing Officer on probation).

(d) *Medical Officer.* Surgeon G H Fink.

Note: **A photograph of the first batch of British Officers is given later.**

Initial Activities and First Battle Honour

The Battalion was stationed at Jalandhar to organize, equip and train. Various procedures were systemized, a sense of esprit de corps was created, and aspects of dedication and discipline inculcated. On 10 March 1891, the Battalion moved from Jalandhar to Delhi, from where after a brief stay it was moved to Manipur to quell disturbances. It did a splendid job there and earned its first Battle Honour 'Manipur', within four years of re-raising. Experienced and proud, it returned to Delhi in September 1894.

Change of Command

Lieutenant Colonel James Cook, after an eventful tenure of seven years, binding the unit as an efficient outfit, relinquished his command on 25 June 1894. The parting words of Lieutenant James Cook were as follows:

> *"As the time approaches which concludes the term of my command of the 36th Sikhs, I feel impelled to place on record my sense of gratitude and keen appreciation of the cheerful assistance, I have throughout received from the*

officers of the Regiment and the ready obedience of all ranks, making the work pleasure and pride. The Regiment being newly formed, coupled with introduction of new drills from time to time, rendered the labours demanded more than ordinarily arduous. I can only express a hope that the labours so honestly bestowed may bring in own award by the advancement of those concerned and the selection of the Corps for Service. In the course of my career, the period I look back on with most pride is that I spent with 36th Sikhs. I need hardly add that I bid you all farewell, Officers, Native Officers, Non-Commissioned Officers and Men, with the deepest regret as having to relinquish a connection with which I have been so intimately wrapt up for the past seven years. I shall watch the onward course of the Corps with keen interest and hope that if it be my lot to be further employed, it may be my great fortune to be associated with my old Regiment, which ever has my best wishes for its welfare in peace or war."

Lieutenant Colonel John Haughton, a soldier par excellence, leader of men, immaculate planner and courageous implementer took over. He had assisted in the raising of 35 Sikhs (later Sikh Regimental Centre). He came at the age of 42 years with service of 24 years that was considered to be early.

35 Sikh (later the Sikh Regimental Centre) was raised along with 36th Sikh in the summer months of 1887, the dress being the same as of 36th Sikhs.

Move to Frontiers

In September 1894, the Unit received orders to move to Peshawar (NWFP). It moved from Delhi on 05 November 1894 by foot to Ludhiana. From there, it entrained to reach Bannu, from where it moved on 11 April 1895 to reach Peshawar on 17 April. It remained there till moved to Kohat reaching there on 19 December 1896. Kohat became springboard for the Regiment. Before their departure, Brigadier General E R Elles CB, inspected the Unit on 20 December 1895, and conveyed his Farewell Order as:

"I am extremely sorry to lose such a fine regiment from my command. Since they have been at Peshawar, the conduct and soldier-like bearing of the Regiment has been in every way excellent and I am well pleased with the Regiment in every respect. As long as we have Regiments like this in the Native Army, we need never be afraid of anything. I hope they may soon have a chance of active service and I wish them every luck where they may be."

On 02 January 1897, the battalion's Right Wing occupied posts at Samana Ridge. The ridge had Khanki Valley to its North and Mirazai Valley in the South. The area was inhabited by Orakazais – who had four main sections – Daulatzai, Ismailzai, Lashkarzai and Hamsaya. The whole clan was split into Samil and Gar.

The Left Wing under Captain W.D. Gordon reached Parchinar on 08 January 1897, having detachments at Thal and Sadda. Parchinar is about 48 miles North-West of Fort Lockhart.

The area Kohat and Kurram border formed a part of responsibility assigned to Major General Yeatman Biggs who was stationed at Hangu, with a total force of a Division of two brigades.

FORT JAMRUD
Built by Hari Singh Nalwa

A Soldier of 36th Sikhs

▲

Soldiers and 'Sardars'
at Samana ▶

British and Native
Officers at Samana

CHAPTER SIX

BATTLE OF SARAGARHI
Holding Out at Samana Ridge

The Topography of Area of Operations

As has been mentioned earlier, the area of NWFP is like the back of an outstretched hand, fingers and knuckles forming ranges and hill tops, extending West to East. It is a dreary limestone area with scanty undergrowth. These ranges are crossable only at passes (*'Kotals'*). The Samana range is formed by a core of limestone-hard like flint. Surface rocks were weather – worn and easy to dig.

The Samana Ridge had Khanki Valley to its North and Miranzai Valley to its South. It is situated 71 degrees longitude and 33 degrees and 30 minutes latitude. Its mean altitude is 6000 feet. Saragarhi fortress is the highest, about 6200 feet. Forts Lockhart and Gulistan are approximately 5000 feet high. Gulistan is located on a saddle, is dominated by observation from Samana Suk, 6743 feet, which is to its North. Lockhart is on a slope and also dominated by observation by heights North and Northwest of it. These two locations were perhaps selected for larger flat areas and availability of water, besides of course, suitable from defence point of view and the possibility garrisoning a large number of troops. The Samana Ridge is 45 miles Southwest of Peshawar, while Kohat is 32 miles to its South. Rawalpindi is 130 miles East of Kohat. Hangu, an important post is 25 miles West of Kohat. Fort Lockhart on Samana Ridge is 25 miles from Hangu. The place is known for severe cold winds during winter.

The Samana Ridge, 12 miles long East to West, then turns Northwards for 35 miles. It is the most suitable defence line from the South to the Frontiers, essential to hold and defend, hence, of interest to the British. From the Western tip, turning Northwards, across the Changru Kotal are the Dargai Heights, which lie in its West. Samana Suk is to its East. There is a road from Shinwari, also a British camp, towards Changru Kotal.

The lower slopes of Samana have low-growing scrub, masses of dwarf palm and intermittent pomegranates. At the time of operations, there was dry grass all around which could be ignited as a force multiplier by either the attacker to generate smoke to move hidden or by the defender deterring the attacker. Water had to be fetched up to the piquets from the springs or rivers using animal transport or at times by the men themselves. All slopes in the Western side had an abundance of trees, which were cut, brought to the picquets and stocked for fire for cooking. The Northern slopes are very gradual, while the Eastern and Western slopes are fairly gradual. The Southern slopes are terribly steep and difficult to negotiate. The Khanki Valley is not as scenic as other valleys in the North.

Military Activities Prior to 1897

In the 1880s and early 1990s, three posts had been established on the Samana Ridge, a fairly flat and broad ridge, to which Orakazais who were occupying the Northern slopes objected. The tribesmen successfully attacked on 04 April forcing the posts to be vacated. It made the British under Brigadier General Sir William Lockhart, launch the Second Miranzai Expedition from 17 April to 05 June 1891. A written agreement was forced on Rabia Khel. Apart from posts already established, additional posts, including Gulistan Fort, were established by 09 May 1891. Fort Lockhart is named after Brigadier General Sir William Lockhart and Gulistan after Sir Louis Cavangiri. The religious leaders of the Afridis and Orakazais, and their representatives, approached the Amir for support to clear Samana but the latter refused.

Forts Gulistan (Cavangiri) and Lockhart (Mastan) were built geometrically rectangular with stone walls of height of twelve to fifteen feet. An enclosure of 80 yards length and 30 yards width were raised around the fort, like 'hornworks'. '*Sangars*' of loose stones were built all around the three walls of the fort while on the fourth side was the fort itself. At places, these hornwork walls were reinforced by flour bags and kerosene tins filled up with loose earth. Some other posts were created to cover the gaps and fringes of the two main forts to ensure a homogenous defence. These were Sartop, Sangar, Dhar and Saragarhi, each with a capacity to hold 25 to 50 men. Smaller posts were also created at Gagra, Lakka, Saifuldara and Tsalai, which were held by a mix of levies and Border Military Force. Southeast of Tsalai was a large post Darband, held by 230 rifles of 3 Sikh under Captain Fasken. The main headquarters with reserves, under Major General Yeatman Biggs, was located at Hangu. The total troops under Biggs were a division which comprised of two brigades with support and logistic elements to defend the area.

Hostilities Swell, Skirmishes Ensue

As said earlier, Tirah erupted due to the imposition of salt tax, encroachment of tribal areas and interference in their customs i.e., imposition of Christianity. On 21 August 1897, information was received that the Orakazais were assembling at Chagru, Sampagha Pass and Khanki valley to attack Samana Ridge, while the Daulatzais were preparing to attack Kohat. Major General Yeatman Biggs, responsible for Kohat-Kurram Border, sent additional ammunition to make up to the tune of 400 rounds per man on Samana posts.

On 25th August, information was received that a large force of Orakazais and Afridis had assembled at Karappa. On 27 August, the Orakzais made a general attack on all the forts and posts of Samana. They had 80 Standards, thus approximately 40,000 fighters in number.

On 28 August, Haughton reinforced Dhar with 37 men. The same day, tribesmen, in great numbers, were observed at Samana Suk, a mile West of Gulistan. Colonel Haughton tried to reinforce Gulistan but found it difficult to do so because of the overwhelming strength of the Pathans, hence decided to engage them from a distance. The Pathans tried to invest Gulistan both from West and East but failed to achieve much because of a very firm and quick reaction from Colonel Haughton and the defenders of Gulistan. Lakka and Saifaldara posts were invested by about 12,000 tribesmen who destroyed and burnt these posts on 29 August. Levies and Border Police did not give ample resistance. The Orakazais ultimately withdrew satisfied that they had been able to destroy at least two posts.

The Orakazais kept up pressure around Samana ridge but without any firm resolve, thus wasted time and opportunity by inconsequential actions like firing from a distance or minor destructive activities of igniting dry grass. The gallant men of the 36th, unmindful of enemy fire ventured out of the forts to put out the fire on the thorn *'abattis'*, a defensive measure taken by Major Des Voeux to thwart any flash charge by the Pathans. Sepoys Sunder Singh and Harnam Singh displayed distinctive acts of valour in voluntarily carrying out these arduous tasks.

On 03 September, a large force of Pathans was seen advancing from Samana Suk towards Gulistan. Colonel Haughton with 50 men advanced to face the situation, leaving 15 men at Saragarhi. The defenders had created another ad hoc measure of piling up wood ahead of hornworks to be lighted in case the tribesmen rushed the fort in the darkness, a possibility always on the cards. The Pathans closed on to Gulistan up to 200 yards. They ignited *'abattis'* (defenders' use of *'panjis'* on ground and sharpened wooden twigs or roots affixed on the fort walls to deter attacker trespass). Two Sepoys from the Fort, Wariam Singh and Gulab Singh volunteered, moved undetected almost amidst the Pathans and quickly put the pile of wood on fire and rushed back unobserved. The tribesmen had amassed all around, raised blood curdling slogans on the beat of tom-toms but the improvisations by the defenders and their gallant reactions deterred the attackers from an assault. They, however, continued similar activities on 4th September too, without making any dent in the defensive arrangement. Disappointed and defeated, they disappeared from the field. Assured the situation was secure, Haughton then withdrew to Lockhart.

Lull and Reinforcements

Thereafter, there was some quiet till 07 September. General Yeatman Biggs, with a force of 2500 men, started from Hangu on 7th September, and reached Fort Lockhart on the 8th. Repairs and reinforcements of the forts were carried out. On the other hand, the Afridis and Orakzais, once again, concentrated in great numbers at Khangarbur on 09 September, 29 'Standards' were counted thus an estimation of about 25,000 tribesmen.

Deception

At this stage, the tribesmen carried out a remarkable deception. On the morning of 11 September, thousands of Pathans with 22 Standards (a flag as a rallying point, representing villages, clans and tribes, generally numbering 100 to 1000 men) moved down the Khanki Valley. To keep a check on any endeavour to act against any post, General Biggs moved parallel to them on the crest of the ridge. At sunset, the Pathans divided themselves into two columns, one returned deceptively up the valley while the other continued Eastwards towards the Khanki Valley. The ruse worked. General Biggs continued Eastwards not knowing about one column of Pathans making a U turn. The British pushed on to Lakha to be able to assist Hangu since an attack was expected there. They in any case were deficient of food and water and required replenishments. The tribesmen took advantage of the situation and on night 11th attacked Sangar. The attack was beaten back. A substantial force of Pathans turned towards Samana on 12 September, duly enforced in great numbers during the night.

Sequence of Events

- 21 August – The Force under General Biggs arrived at Kohat.
- 25 August – Orakazais drove cows in front of their advance to a watch post, the Sikh defenders refrained from firing, and were trapped by the wily Pathans.
- 27 August – Gulistan was invested by the Pathans without any results. Same day, however, Lakha and Saifudara police posts were destroyed.
- 28 August – Sangar and Dar posts were invested. Kyhber police evacuated Gogra and Tsalai posts without giving a fight.
- 03 September – Gulistan fort was invested and attacked.
- 04 September – Afridis joined Orakazais.
- 08 September – Kurram and Kohat forces arrived. General Biggs reinforced posts at Samana.
- 11 September – Force returned to Hangu. Deceptive move by the tribesmen effected. Sangar was attacked at night.
- 12 September – Gulistan, Saragarhi, Sangar and Dar were attacked. Lockhart was cut off from sending any reinforcements. Main fury was at Saragarhi.

Deployment on Samana Ridge

The deployment at Samana Ridge on 12 September was as follows:

- Fort Lockhart – 168 men under Lieutenant Colonel J Haughton and Lieutenant Munn, the adjutant, a daredevil subaltern of three years service. There were also present two attached officers Lieutenant Lillie of the Irish Rifles and Lieutenant Haslam of the Royal Engineers. Mrs Haughton was also present till the beginning of the hostilities but had to leave for England because of the illness of her mother.

- Fort Gulistan – 175 men under Major Des Voeux and Second Lieutenant HRE Pratt. The doctor present was Surgeon Captain CB Prall. Another officer Lieutenant AK Blair was wounded and lying in the hospital. (Mrs Des Voeux with her children and nurse Teresa Mc Grath were also present at the post during the attacks on Saragarhi and Gulistan). There were two Indian officers at the fort – Subedar Dewan Singh and Jemadar (now Naib Subedar) Jwala Singh.
- Saragarhi – 21 men and a Non Combatant Employee (NCE)
- Dhar – 27 men.
- Sangar – 44 men.
- Saratop – 24 men.
- Crag – 22 men.

The above figures exclude the figures of followers who must have been on all the posts, their records were not mentioned. Saragarhi Post had 21 combatants and one follower, by the name of Dad.

Note: A sketch showing deployment of 36th Sikhs at Samana is enclosed.

Saragarhi Post

Saragarhi, '*Sara*' is a Pashtoon word in its literal sense means 'red' and '*garhi*' 'small fort'. An historian has claimed that 'Sara' was the name of Prophet Hazrat Mohmmad. It was prepared to hold up to 50 men. It was one and half miles West of Lockhart and one and three quarters' mile East of Gulistan. As the crow flies, the distance between the forts was long and there was the intervening feature Saragarhi, rendering direct communication between the two difficult. Saragarhi was thus established as an intercommunication post, which also had tremendous tactical significance as it covered the physical gap between the two forts. It was assailable from three spurs from North, Northeast and East, all meeting a little distance from the main entrance. An assault from any direction, however, was subject to interference from the two main forts. But once taken over, provided a suitable ground to attack any of the two main forts. The communication was carried out with the help of a heliograph. Also, flags during day (semaphore), and lanterns at night were put to use. The post had twenty one soldiers and a non-combatant. The soldiers were of Jat Sikh community from Punjab. They all were of a sturdy physique and were strong willed, fond of playing *'kabaddi'* and drinking, under a Non Commissioned Officer, Havildar Ishar Singh. The defenders fought under the indomitable and inspiring leadership of their post commander, knowing well that their fort was more or less a make-shift construction of arranged stones and mud walls with a wooden door that could not withstand an onslaught of hundreds.

Havildar Ishar Singh

Havildar Ishar Singh was of tough exterior, a man of determination and a hard task master. He was of an independent easy going nature, tuned to military life, often confronted superiors and perhaps, thus not found fit for further promotion. But his single leadership qualities and stuborn doggedness won him the confidence of his superiors to bestow him with the command of an important post. With his exemplary courage, he roused his wards to give their best. His personal example of what a soldier shows as a warrior in the true sense is aptly described as:

> *"A leader is the one who knows the way, goes the way, and shows the way."*
>
> – John C Maxwell

Heliography

It is a technique invented in the 19th century, using sunrays/sunlight to send messages through Morse code. The expression is derived from latin words 'helio' and 'graphic' meaning 'sun' and 'writing' respectively. It had many versions; one used by the British Army was Mance Mark V. The flashes were produced by momentarily pivoting the mirror, or by interrupting the beam with a shutter. The messages were sent without cables, using sunlight falling on mirrors, forming different patterns of flashlights denoting set words and war situations. This was in ample use during that period.

The technique had the advantage of long distance communications (tested in India for 35 miles) without any heavy fixed structure, it was portable 07 lbs in weight, not requiring a power source and secure since the beam was narrow and thus averse to any interruption unless tried close to the beam and someone knowing the code. There were, of course, disadvantages of dependence on sun rays and requirement of a clear line of sight.

The Battle

On 12th morning, a bright day, thousands invaded Gulistan and also surrounded Lockhart to obstruct any help from there, while a major force concentrated to eliminate Saragarhi. *'Lashkars'* were observed near Gogra and Samana Suk.

The Pathans surrounded the Post by 8 am. The first assault was launched at 9 am. With a great sense of fire discipline, Havildar Ishar Singh held back fire till the Pathans closed in and were well within the rifle range and he then let out an intense volley on the enemy. The Sikhs had Martini Henry breach loading rifles that fired 10 rounds per minute, more than a match to those with the Pathans. The first assault by the Pathans was repulsed with severe punishment to them. The Sikhs though were guarding all around but most were concentrated to face the main attack. They had taken up positions lying on the ground where feasible to bring in effective fire, kneeling or standing, ensuring best use of slots in the walls. This was done to bring about a concentrated fusillade of intense fire on the attackers. Dozens of Afridis died or were severely wounded. Their attack failed, they ran helter-skelter, some hiding behind the boulders and in the dips and fringes in the ground. Hidden, they kept up the pressure on the defenders through sustained fire. The Pathans attacked yet again but failed. Their leader Gul Badshah tried to threaten the defenders by making announcements that they cannot fight against so many and shall die ultimately. He tried to dissuade them from their task asking they were fighting another's battle? He also lured them with tempting promises that if they surrendered, they will be looked after and allowed to go back safely. The high morale of the defenders was evident from their full-throated blood-curdling *'Jaikaras'* (war cries), *'Bole so Nihal, Sat Sri Akal'*, from all the forts and posts.

The defenders under a, steadfast and stubborn leader gave them rebuttal, time and again, verbally as well as physically. It is known that Havildar Ishar Singh gave a mouthful diatribe in reply to Pathan Gul

Badshah's alluring attempt. But for how long? The strength at Saragarhi was dwindling under the ferocious impact of wave after wave of blood thirsty marauding tribesmen, incited with religious. By 11 am, Sepoys Bhagwan Singh and Naik Lal Singh were wounded, succumbing to their grievous wounds. Buta Singh and Sunder Singh followed sacrificing their lives. By now, the Pathans had lost well over a hundred of men. The lessened strength of the defenders and time taken to reload the rifles impeded their effort to keep the enemy at bay, resulting in the outcome of the battle changing hands in favour of the tribesmen.

The tribesmen had also put to use their practiced trick to ignite dry bushes and scrubs around a piquet and move forward unseen behind the smoke. After initial attacks, they had left men with a charpoy covered with earth and pebbles, lifted over their heads protecting them from the defender's bullets to get near to a safe place along the wall where they started puncturing a hole in it. They made use of a snag in the construction of the post, whereby there was a dip that could not be watched and covered by the defenders. This was well seen from Fort Gulistan, Major Des Voeux tried to warn, but perhaps either the message could not be seen or understood or the defenders were unable to do anything about it being at a dead angle.

No help could be forthcoming from Lockhart since it was virtually besieged. An effort by Lieutenant Munn with some men taking positions outside the fort trying to divert the attacker's attention by fire, did not achieve much. The tribesmen also used already prepared bundles of dry grass throwing them forward like fagots, burning them and moving behind the smoke. All that Colonel Haughton could do was to advise the Saragarhi defenders to conserve ammunition, such was his concern and knowledge of the tactical and logistic situation. Each soldier had 100 rounds with him and 300 as reserve.

Another snag in the construction of the fort was noticed after the battle which was that the main door was made of wood and had not been strengthened with nails. It gave way into shards by volleys and volleys of bullets from muzzle-loading Jezail rifles and the Martinis that the tribesmen possessed. By 3 pm, even the ammunition with the few Sikhs that were left, finished and they had to resort to hand to hand fight. Sepoys Sahib Singh, Jiwan Singh and Dya Singh died while fighting with bayonets to stop the Pathans entering the Post.

The breach made by the hidden tribesmen had been enlarged to almost seven feet high and twelve feet wide (this is what was found later when the fortress was destroyed, so the gap could have been less when the Pathans actually entered), enough opening for the attackers to swarm in numbers and overwhelm the few defenders who were surviving and who took to their bayonets and swords. The defenders killed many before succumbing to their grievous wounds. Sepoy Gurmukh Singh, the signaler, deserves a special mention since he sent messages like reduced strength, requesting for ammunition and reinforcements, and ultimately seeking permission to destroy the heliograph, picked up his rifle and killed almost twenty of the enemy before falling when wounded several times. His fight was an essence culmination of eventual fulfillment of responsibility and duty. At this stage once again, Colonel Haughton took about 90 soldiers along with two officers to assist the Saragarhi defenders, but what he saw was that all was finished, with hundreds of Pathans swarming into the little fortress. The Pathans ignited the post, soon the wooden rafters caught fire and crumbled down. The uneven battle had taken almost seven hours, such was the tenacity of the few against ferocious thousands.

It is also known that non-combatant Daad, who obviously had learnt how to fire a rifle, had taken to one and killed a few attackers before laying down his life along with his colleagues. He thus carried out his dual responsibility, initially opening ammunition boxes, and supplying ammunition to the soldiers, providing water to them and looking after the wounded, he fought to the last and died a martyr.

It would be interesting to mention that the same policy of providing preliminary training to non-combatants continued even after partition. In the Indo-China War in 1962, a Havildar boot-maker Kirpa Ram of 4 Sikh had volunteered and goaded other non-combatants to volunteer to carry ammunition boxes from the base, 6000 feet up, to the defences. During a later effort he got involved in fighting with the Chinese, killed some, before succumbing to his increasing wounds. It is a record that he was awarded the Vir Chakra posthumously. There are also examples of non-combatants of the unit duly awarded during the Second World War. Number 95 water carrier Rattan Singh was decorated for devotion to duty at Eritrea with a Mention-in-Despatches and another NCE being awarded with an IDSM. The irony, is that a non-combatant during the Battle of Sargarhi, was not duly awarded, in spite of the chivalry he displayed.

The battle continued for almost the whole day as the Pathans kept on maneuvering to better positions and were trying to exhaust the defenders. Besides, several attacks launched by them had to be repulsed that consumed ammunition which slowly got depleted. As was witnessed, the Pathans wreaked a barbarous vengeance on some of the dead mutilating their bodies. They threw burning faggots and destroyed by fire whatever could be burnt. Later, the tribesmen themselves had given a figure of their 200 dead and 600 wounded. While figures given by Gul Badshah himself later were 180-200 dead, the relief column had found it to be 600 and above, a fair guess therefore can easily be assumed. And that is what was achieved by just 22 defenders.

Aftermath

The Pathans attacked Sangar on 13 and 14 September, but were pushed back. They attacked Fort Gulistan but were defeated there too, the troops manning their posts for an agonising 50 hours continuously. The Pathans had planted their standards on the walls of the fort. Firing continued throughout the night. Major Des Voeux detailed a posse of 16 men under Havildar Kala Singh who charged the *'sangars'* occupied by the Pathans and cleared them from the South-West corner.

On the spur of the moment, Havildar Sunder Singh with about 11 men leapt out of their defences and charged the enemy joining hands with Havildar Kala Singh's party. They killed and injured many of the enemy, making the remaining flee from the field. The forging parties were detailed to follow them, inflict casualties and rout them. Half of the forging parties were also wounded. On their return to the ramparts they found two of their comrades missing. Three soldiers of those had just returned went back and came back with their two missing colleagues, who were wounded; such was the valour and esprit de corps. In the process they captured three Afghan standards. There were casualties on both sides, the position remained unaltered as far as defence of the fort was concerned, the Pathans trying to keep up the pressure throughout the night of 13/14 September.

Meanwhile, General Biggs force drove out the Pathans from Gogra, Dhar and Sangar by 10 am on 14 September. The firing of the screw guns on 13 and 14 had a statutory effect making the Pathans recoil to safety. Relief reached Gulistan by 1 pm. The Pathans under pressure of shelling withdrew towards Samana Suk. They had four hundred killed and more than six hundred wounded. All the forts were repaired and snags attended to. The garrison at Sangar had also made a sortie and had captured a 'Standard' which they displayed to General Biggs Force with the heart filling slogan *'Bole so Nihal, Sat Sri Akal'*. A reconnaissance on 16 September revealed the Pathans had dropped their efforts of any further adventure at Samana and had dispersed from there.

It was during the night of intense fighting that Mrs Des Voeux gave birth to a baby girl, who was christened Samana. The nurse Teresa McGarth did a splendid job of looking after the lady, the newborn and the wounded soldiers. Her efforts were duly recognized with the award of 'Indian Frontier Medal with Clasp for 1897 Samana', and Her Majesty bestowing her with the medal of 'Royal Red Cross.'

The Impact

Without the stiff resistance of the 'Twenty One', other piquets or the main forts would have been in the line of attack by the Afghans in a 'do or die' resolution. The importance of the forts lay in the fact that elimination of even one would have given the Pathans a foothold with costly eviction later, if at all. The 'Twenty One' fought long enough gaining crucial time for the relief columns to reach.

The defenders, all of 36 Sikhs, had displayed remarkable grit and determination on the entire Samana ridge, against relentless Pathans whose resolve to punish the defenders and clear the ridge from their occupation was exemplary. However, the unflinching loyalty and valour of the Sikhs under their fine leaders, Colonel Haughton at the higher level and the likes of Havildar Ishar Singh at a lower level was a shining paradigm. The bravery by the martyrs at the little post of Saragarhi who faced the main brunt of the Pathan onslaught was iconic.

The battle can be concluded as a tactical victory of a minor magnitude for the Pathans but a strategic victory of the British Indian troops, the Sikhs. 36th Sikhs in its gallant actions of holding out at Samana suffered thirty killed and forty one wounded.

Honours and Awards

Lieutenant Colonel John Haughton was the first to recognize the bravery of the martyrs. He saluted facing the Saragarhi Post. The news spread soon all over. The Punjab Governor recognized the brave act and immediately conveyed it to England. The British Parliament happened to be in session. On hearing of the act of unparallel bravery, steadfastness, utmost loyalty and supreme sacrifice, all the Members Parliament stood up, paid homage and gave a standing ovation that had never happened before. Parliament of the United Kingdom passed the following remark, vide "The London Gazette," Publication date: 11 February 1898, Issue 26937, p. 863:

> *"The British, as well as the Indians, are proud of the 36th Sikh Regiment. It is no exaggeration to record that the armies which possess the valiant Sikhs cannot face defeat in war."*

Hearing the story, Queen Victoria, announced the award of Indian Order of Merit Class II to all the 21 combatants who had faced unprecedented odds. The award was then the highest presented to the native soldiers. It was thus accepted by the British Government that it was equivalent of Victoria Cross, highest award given to British soldiers.

The descendants of the Saragarhi heroes were awarded Rs 500 in cash and two 'murrabas' of land each, equivalent to 50 acres. 12 September was declared a holiday to all regiments and battalions having Sikh troops on their roll. There were glittering accolades from Major General Yeatman Biggs, who on the conclusion of the battle had this to say, *"I hope that the loyalty and bravery of twenty one Sikhs would be recorded in golden letters in British military history."*

An extract from G.O.M.D. 1417, Fort William, 24 Dec 1997: *"...The Governor General in Council desires to express his admiration of the brilliant defence ... who died fighting to the last, displaying a heroic devotion which has never been surpassed in the annals of the Indian Army.... Fighting against overwhelming odds, they died at the post, thus proving the loyalty and devotion to their sovereign, while upholding to the last, the traditional bravery of the Sikh nation..."*.

The then Punjab Government raised a Cairn out of the stones of the fortress at the site of the battle (which has with time disintegrated and in ruins now), a memorial at Samana in November 1901 and Saragarhi Gurudawara at Amritsar was unveiled on 14 February 1902. (*Today it forms a part of the galleria/plaza approaching the Golden Temple, with a recently built imposing Saragarhi Sarai' in the back ground*).

The 'Pioneer' newspaper from Lucknow, collected a large sum of money and got the Saragarhi Memorial Gurudawara constructed at Ferozepur since maximum Saragarhi heroes hailed from that district. It was inaugurated in 1904 by Sir Charles Pevz, the Lieutenant Governor of Punjab. The District at that time happened to be one of the biggest including today's districts of Ferozepur, Moga, Faridkot, Fazilka and large areas around.

A Memorial was also erected at the old Sikh Regimental Centre at Meerut during the time of Major General V R Khanolkar as Colonel of the Regiment and Lieutenant Colonel Budh Singh, MC, the Centre Commandant. Another one was erected at the new location of the Sikh Regimental Centre at Ramgarh Cantt, Hazaribagh in 1992 (an initiative of the author when he was the Commandant). In 1971, an Indian War Memorial was inaugurated by Field Marshal Claude Aukinleck at the Royal Military Academy, Sandhurst, Surrey. There are also Memorials of Havildar Ishar Singh at Village Jhorran, in District Ludhiana and of Naik Lal Singh in village Dhun Dhai Wala in District Tarartarn, with the initiatives of the descendents of the martyrs and villagers, and with some help from the Sikh Regimental Centre, 4 Sikh and personnel of the Sikh Regiment, especially 3 Sikh (XLV) RATTRAY) Veterans Welfare Association, an initiative of Colonel Karaminder Singh.

The commemorative tablet at the site raised by the British has the following inscription:

> *"The Government of India has caused this tablet to be erected in the memory of the twenty one non commissioned officers and men of the 36 Sikh Regiment of the Bengal Infantry whose names are engraved below as a perpetual record of the heroism shown by these gallant soldiers who died at their posts in defence of the fort of Saragarhi, on 12th September 1897, fighting against overwhelming numbers, thus proving their loyalty and devotion to their sovereign, the Queen Empress of India, and gloriously maintaining the reputation of the Sikhs for unflinching courage on the field of battle."*

165 Havildar Ishar Singh

332 Naik Lal Singh
546 Lance Naik Chanda Singh
1321 Sepoy Sundar Singh
287 " Ram Singh

834 Sepoy Narayan Singh
814 " Gurmukh Singh
871 " Jivan Singh
1733 " Gurmukh Singh

492	*"*	*Uttar Singh*	*163*	*"*	*Ram Singh*
182	*"*	*Sahib Singh*	*1257*	*"*	*Bhagwan Singh*
359	*"*	*Hira Singh*	*1265*	*"*	*Bhagwan Singh*
687	*"*	*Daya Singh*	*1556*	*"*	*Buta Singh*
760	*"*	*Jivan Singh*	*1651*	*"*	*Jivan Singh*
791	*"*	*Bhola Singh*	*1221*	*"*	*Nand Singh*

Doctor Zakir Hussain, the ex Governor of Bihar, later President of India, said about the Battle of Saragarhi:

> *"On this fateful day, on a rugged, inhospitable ridge of forbidding terrain, a brave little band of twenty one Sikhs stood its ground steadfastly to the utter last, in the midst of swarming sea of hostile assailants, and bore unmistakable witness to the gallantry and honour of the Indian Army. It is an episode that we remember today, but it is nonetheless a historic event in the annals of our history, rich with lessons of unsurpassed gallantry, self-effacing loyalty and unconditional allegiance to the call of duty."*

Martyrs – Present day Descendants and Heirs

36th Sikhs was raised on 23 March 1887. To be recruited for the army, an age group of 17 to 20 years was fixed for the aspiring candidates. Thus it can be assessed that the first group at the time of the Battle of Saragarhi must have been in the age group of 27 to 30 years, and the second group 24 to 29 years. Havildar Ishar Singh was already serving in the Bengal Infantry. The numbers of the seniors in 36th Sikhs were Sepoy Ram Singh 163, Havildar Ishar Singh 165, Sepoy Sahib Singh 182 and Naik Lal Singh 332. It can be presumed Havildar Ishar Singh, Naik Lal Singh, Sepoy Ram Singh and Sepoy Sahib Singh must have been 35 to 40 years old.

Note: Order of briefs of doscendants is given as rank holders and then as per seniority in number.

Shaheed Havildar Ishar Singh (165)

He was born in village Jhoraarn, Raikot in Jagraon Tehsil of Ferozepur District in 1858. He joined the Punjab Frontier Force in 1876 at the age of 19. He became a Havildar in 1892, a rank in which he joined XXXVI Sikhs. He was given the charge of Saragarhi Post on 02 January in 1897.

His father was Sardar Dhaula Singh who had two brothers Sardar Mehna Singh and Sardar Didar Singh. Ishar Singh had an elder brother

Nagar Singh. Ishar Singh married Jiwani Kaur in 1893. But from 1894 to 1897, that is till he died he remained on duty at Peshawar and Samana. His wife died some time later without an issue. Among his descendants, he now has his paternal uncle's first generation Bikkar Singh who is of unstable mind and lives in village Jhorran with his son. Havildar Bakhtawar Singh (ex 17 Sikh), Son of Sardar Didar Singh, paternal uncle of Ishar Singh has been adopted and nominated as owner of the property as descendant of Havildar Ishar Singh. He lives in village Satowal, Raikot, Ludhiana. His brother Amandeep Singh lives in Patiala.

Shaheed Naik Lal Singh (332)

He was born in 1857, son of Sardar Hari Singh of village Dhun Dhai Wala, Block Chohla Sahib in Taran Tarn. He was married to Bibi Prem Kaur. They had a son who died. Prem Kaur lived for 57 years. Lal Singh was an outstanding wrestler. He had been recruited by Homes, after a wrestling duel. His family and the villagers have raised a Memorial at his home at Dhun. Land awarded to him is divided among descendants Manjit Singh, Charanjit Singh, Satnam Singh, Sarabjit Singh, Harkirat Singh, who live at Nakodar, Jagraon.

Shaheed Lance Naik Chanda Singh (546)

He was the youngest among four brothers, sons of Sardar Rattan Singh. Chanda Singh was born in 1868. At the age of 17, he joined the PFF. He was promoted on the raising of 36 Sikhs. He was married to Sant Kaur, who on his martyrdom married his elder brother Ganga Singh.

Shaheed Ram Singh (163)

Son of Sardar Sohan Singh of village Kandhla, Jalandhar; further details not known.

Shaheed Sahib Singh (182)

No information is available.

Shaheed Ram Singh (287)

Son of Sardar Bhagwan Singh; no further information available.

Shaheed Hira Singh (359)

His father Sardar Bara Singh belonged to Moga, Ferozepur. Hira Singh was born in 1871, at village Dulo Roola in Mintgomery. He was married to Bibi Inder Kaur. At the time of his martyrdom, his daughter Gujjari Kaur was three months old whom he never saw. Third generation Gurmail Singh and Charan Singh live in the village.

Shaheed Uttam Singh (492)

He was born in 1872 son of Sardar Lehna Singh Gill of Moga, Ferozepur. His elder brother Sardar Gurmukh Singh was allotted land. The family, third generation, a large family continues to live in villages Harayu and Gandhuan.

Shaheed Daya Singh (687)

He was born in 1870 in the house of Sardar Sangat Singh at Kharak Singh Wala, Patiala. Whereabouts of descendants are not known.

Shaheed Jivan Singh (760)

Son of Sardar Hira Singh, was born at village Sangatpura, Jallundur. Further information about descendants is not known.

Shaheed Bhola Singh (791)

His year of birth was 1865, other details are not known.

Shaheed Gurmukh Singh (814)

He was born in 1870. His father Sardar Rann Singh and mother Gul Kaur belonged to village Dhamdour, district Jalandhur. Rann Singh had seven sons and one daughter. His sons Kishan Singh and Genda Singh lived in the village.

Shaheed Narayan Singh (834)

He was born in the house of Sardar Gujar Singh of village Bassi, Patiala. He had a beloved whom he could not marry as the fate ordained differently. His older brother Sewa Singh was given land in Layalpur. Their fifth generation Arjan Singh and family are now settled at Kutba, District Patiala.

Shaheed Jivan Singh (871)

Son of Sardar Nuppa Singh, village Dhumanda, Jalandhar.

Shaheed Nand Singh (1221)

Born in 1873, he was a Sehajdhari (cut their hair but have faith in Sikhism). His father Shri Devi Datta was from village Atowal, Hoshiarpur. Devi Datta inspired his sons Nand Singh, Uttam Singh and Chanda Singh to be baptized to Sikhism by having *'Amrit'*. Nand Singh was betrothed in 1893, but before his marriage could be solemnized, he moved to Peshawar. He died at the age of 24 years.

Shaheed Bhagwan Singh (1257)

Son of Sardar Hira Singh, from village Lohgarh, Amargarh, Patiala.

Shaheed Bhagwan Singh (1265)

Son of Sardar Vir Singh, born in village Mubhewala, Ludhiana. Further whereabouts are not known.

Shaheed Sunder Singh (1321)

Son of Sardar Sudh Singh of village Balia, Ludhiana; further details are not known.

Shaheed Buta Singh (1556)

Son of Sardar Charat Singh, village Sherpur, Phillaur, Jalandhar; whereabouts of descendants not known.

Shaheed Jivan Singh (1651)

He was born in Guri, Phillaur, District Jallundur, in 1871, as son of Sardar Kirpal Singh Dhariwal. He had two brothers Sunder Singh and Samund Singh. Jiwan Singh died at the age of 26 years. He had a son Bhola Singh who was two and half years old when Jiwan Singh was martyred. Jiwan Singh had not even seen his son. Bhola Singh married Ram Kaur in 1921. They now live in village Mauli, Phagwara.

Shaheed Gurmukh Singh (Signalman) (1733)

He hailed from village Chulliwal, Nakodar, Jalandhar. He was born in 1834 His father was Sardar Garja Singh. His elder brothers were Mota Singh, Kirpa Singh, Rode Singh and Kaku Singh. He was unmarried. After the partition of India and Pakistan, his descendant Mansa Singh settled at Ludhiana. His other nephew Jawala Singh and some other relatives live in different places.

Non-Combatant Dadh

His whereabouts are not known. Even his actual name is not clear – Dadh Singh or Khuda Dadh. It was assumed he belonged to Naushehra in Jammu and Kashmir, and later moved to Pakistan at the time of partition. However, as per the latest information, March 2018, by Captain Amarinder Singh, CM Punjab, a historian of great repute and authenticity, the local myth in the village is that name Dadh belonged to two local persons, who were employed at Saragarhi, one inside and the other outside. Inside was Karamdaad. They both had been asked by the Orakazai tribe who knew them to walk away, but instead both men sided with their Sikh brothern. Numerous guesses have been made whether he was a sweeper, cook or *'bishti'* (one who fetches water), with added task of carrier of messages in emergency, perhaps all rolled in one though there may have been reservations for employment as a cook if he was a sweeper (now designated safaiwala). In that case, cooking would have been done by one or two of the soldiers themselves as always was the case in smaller outfits. There is no doubt that Dadh would have been trained to bare essential fundamentals of combat to rise to the occasion for self-defence or as the situation demanded.

Note: The battle was observed from both the forts, Lockhart and Gulistan, but being surrounded themselves, could not help the tiny post. The eye-witnessed entire story is narrated by Lieutenant Colonel John Haughton Commanding Officer, which is written in Chapter Eight.

"I am, now, in celestial peace,
bliss, and joyful pleasure
and wonderous is my Glory"

– Guru Granth Sahib

Orakazai Country

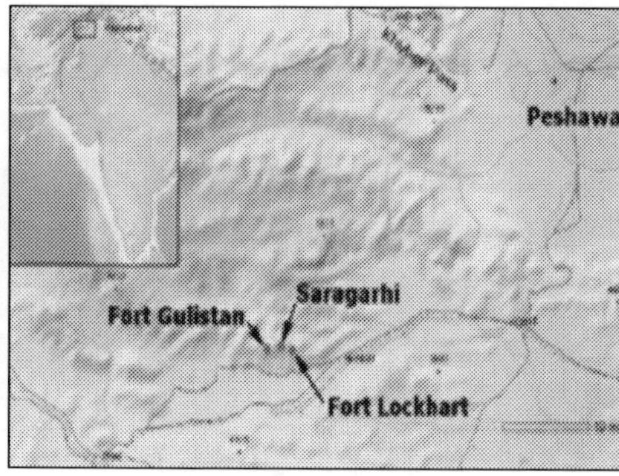

Location of Forts
(Google Image)

Fort Lockhart

Fort Gulistan

View of Saragarhi Fort
From Fort Lockhart

View of Saragarhi Fort
From Fort Gulistan

Map Illustrating
Deployment 36 Sikhs and other Troops at Samana Ridge

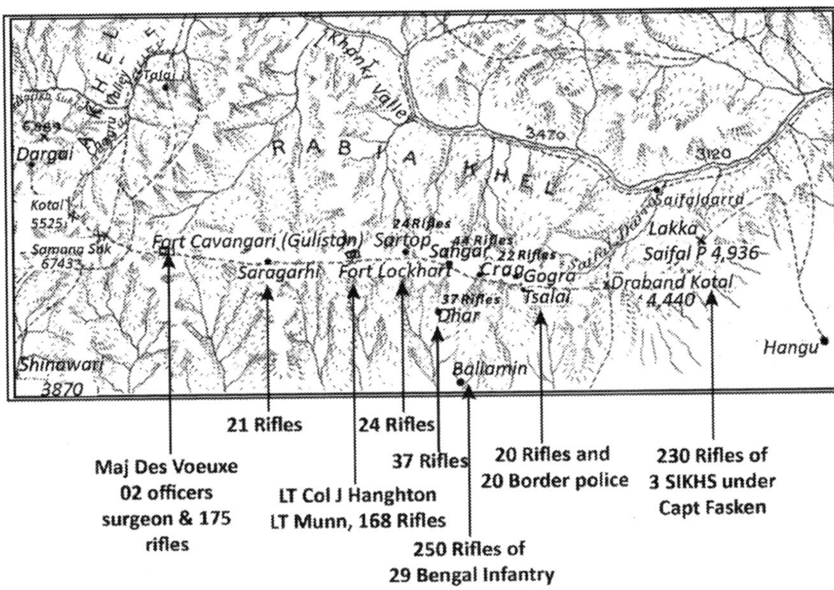

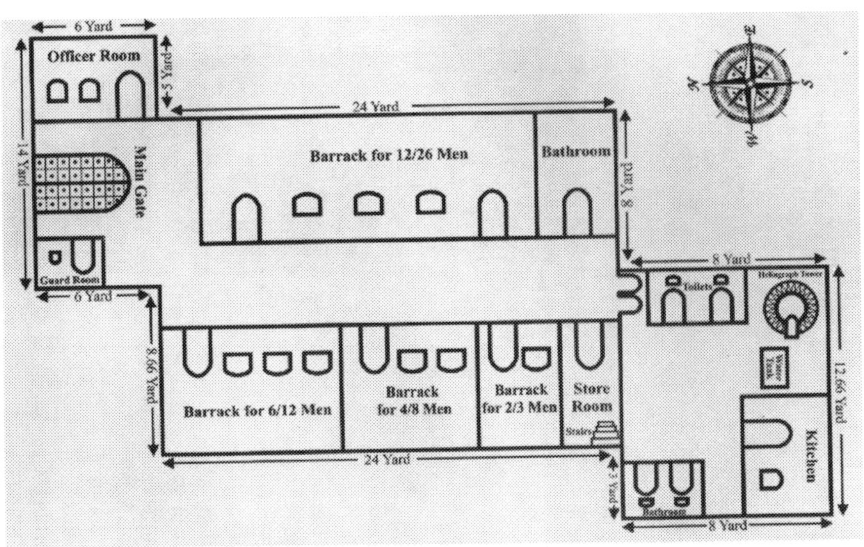

Original Plan of Saragarhi Post Main Block

Pathway to Saragarhi

Intervening Country between Saragarhi and Fort Lockhart

Ruins of Saragarhi Post after its Capture

Breach Through which Afridis swarmed in

First sortie by Havildar Kala Singh and 16 men at 0800 hrs

Second sortie by Havildar Sundar Singh and eleven men at 0810 hrs to Kala Singh's assistance

36th Sikhs' Proud Possession
Captured three Afridi Flags

Accepted image of Havildar Ishar Singh

The Memorial at Saragarhi Location

Cairn on the Site of Saragarhi Fort

Pathan who claimed to have fought against XXXVI during battle of Saragarhi

Epitaph on the Saragarhi Memorial

Saragarhi Award Flag

Gurudwara Amritsar

Gurudwara Ferozepur

CHAPTER SEVEN

THE TIRAH CAMPAIGN 1897-98

No Winner No Loser

"'Mid dark ravines, by precipices vast,
Did there and here your dreadful conflict sway."

– Archbishop Trench

General

A study of wars is not only to record incidents, actions and battles in chronological order but to also visualize the factors that lead to blood shedding and its aftermath. Thus the study would be incomplete unless a battle or campaign is examined in its totality, viz background history, geography and climate, people who fought or were involved in one way or the other, international influences, economy, social fibre, tactics, strategy, weapons, equipment and other force-multipliers.

36th Sikhs had moved to the Frontier in September 1894, occupied the Samana posts on 02 January 1897, fought to defend the ridge, was retained in the Tirah area to fight many more battles and was withdrawn only on conclusion of the Tirah Campaign in April 1898. Its contribution would thus be an essential part of the situation and psyche of the time. Since 36th Sikhs was a successor of 14th Ferozepur Sikhs (1 Sikh, now 4 Mechanised), 15th Ludhiana Sikhs (2 Sikh) and contemporary of 35th Sikhs (The Sikh Regimental Centre) and 45th Rattaray's Sikhs (3 Sikh), reference of the gallant units shall form part of the narrative. This, however, does not diminish in any way, the magnificent part played by other infantry, cavalry and artillery units, not to forget the highly worthy part played by the logistics units. To study the finale of the British adventure, therefore, on the Frontier forms an essential part as the forces that fought were a mix of regiments of numerous origins that included Gurkhas, Punjab Frontier Force, Bengal Infantry and Levies, Muslims, Sikhs and so on.

The British were infuriated by the betrayal of the tribesmen, on charges to some extent, they had themselves perpetrated. They deduced that the Afridis and Orakazais had faltered intentionally on the agreements made sixteen years earlier. They further felt that the aggressive actions by the tribesmen were unprovoked and the damages done by them to the British territories and subjects were punishable offences. There lay the crux of substantiating the *'forward policy'*.

The *'Great Game'* of moving forward to checkmate the French and the Russians once subsided, the threat was felt to be lesser, changed to a policy of annexation to expand the 'Raj'. The seeds of discord with the Afghans, that had been sown by way of drawing the Durand Line in 1893, proved to be reason for trouble. The British wanted clear-cut boundaries and the Amir was drawn into it for assurances to help him retain his seat. This did not go well with the tribesmen, who accepted no authority except dictates of their own Maliks and Mullas. They could not relish the divisions of their land. Their natural urge, ever eagerness for excursions, and spirit for independence from any rules pushed them to rise. However, many Britishers have painted them badly.

The tribals accepted the Amir when it suited them and so was the case in their dealings with the British. They objected to the Durand Line between Afghanistan and India. The Amir himself though signed the accord, yet was skeptical to the idea of a boundary. It took much goading, patience, tact and a bit of coercion by Sir Mortimer Durand to make the Amir sign. All the parties except the British felt that everything was going on smoothly so why draw borders. The Amir considered the tribesmen as an independent entity, a safe bet for himself. He understood that the British were resilient to implement what they achieved, if one line that restricted the other side from trespassing for whatever reason, another line was always in the offing to further checkmate them.

On the other hand, the British have justified that they had always abided by the agreements. Unwittingly and admittedly – the two mixed contradictions – in Frontiers, they slowly and steadily improved their own positions and whenever circumstances were favourable they made advances to make their positions secure. They pushed forward their posts, made roads, tracks, and reinforced garrisons. They even intervened in local affairs, enforced their ideas, advanced to absorb, dominate, gain administrative control and perhaps tried to spread Christianity.

The Amir did realize the above. He had his own apprehensions and woes that the British will ultimately overcome all problems of crossing the mountains and make inroads to Kabul. Notwithstanding this, the marking of the Durand Line was undertaken. The British provided a strong escort of 3000 men and 6 guns. The task was started from South of Waziristan. The tribesmen showed their resentment by a fierce attack at the British camp at Wana on 03 November 1894. As a reprisal, an expedition was undertaken under Sir William Lockhart who punished the tribesmen inflicting destruction till they were subdued and made to pay fines. The boundary was duly marked from Gomel in the South to Kurram in the North. Though the tribesmen accepted boundary pillars drawn into the earth, willy-nilly, but felt these were inemical to their interests. Concurrently, military posts were established at Wana, Gomel, Tochi, Kurram Valley, Samana range, Chitral, Malakand and Chakdara.

When the boundary was demarcated North of Khyber, even the Amir's forces assisted. However, in 1895, an incident occurred at Chitral. The British immediately took a military expedition which succeeded in its mission. As a consequence, a fort was erected at Chitral and strong posts were established at Malakand and Chakdara. To absorb the locals, the tribesmen were given employment, though they remained apprehensive of further manoeuvers by the British. In June 1897, the political officer and his escort were attacked at Tochi. On 26 July 1897, about 20,000 tribesmen attacked Malakand and Chakdara. 45 Sikhs carried out a magnificent feat at Malakand, defending the post against an attack by thousands of Afghans.

Meanwhile, the Amir's Sipah Salar, Ghulam Hyder Khan, a strong man of influence, connived with the Mullas – Sayid Akbar of Aka Khels, 'Mad Fakir' of Swat and Najmat-ud-din of Hadda at Jarobi in Mohamand country. The Amir also sympathized with them, though not openly. In fact, the Amir had written a book *'Taqwin-ud-din'* which propagated war of religious fanatics i.e., *'Jihad'*. Accordingly, the tribesmen were motivated by the spirit of Islam to wage wars against the infidels. The Amir also, assumed the title of *'Zia-ul Millat-wa-ud-din'*, meaning the 'Light of Union and Faith', thus proclaiming himself to be the 'King of Islam'. At the same time, a Turkish visitor was received at Kabul to the chagrin of the British. These incidents were followed by an outburst, thus giving an impression that these were nurtured and were interlinked. Ironically, the Amir denied that he had anything to do with the uprisings. The argument was accepted by the authorities, though not convincingly.

The Mad Mulla claimed himself to be the successor, and divine selection, of the late Akhund of Swat, and played upon the veneration that the tribesmen had for him. He sermonized that actions by the British were provocative and thus the Afghans must defend their interest against 'Annexation by the Infidel.' The Mulla had seized the opportunity and succeeded in working upon the fanaticism of the tribesmen. He appeared in Upper Swat in July 1897, and gradually worked his way to the valley.

Grievances of the Afridis

The Afridis alleged the reasons for their resentment as encroachment of their country, increase in salt tax and interference in their customs to include non-return of their women who had taken refuge in British territories.

After the Afghan War 1878-80, the British had agreed with the Afridis to keep open the important Khyber Pass open. For the protection of the area, the Afridis levies were given responsibility. The Afridis were paid Rs 87,000 annually for the arrangement to keep the pass open. The Amir also agreed, since he benefitted by getting tolls from caravans that traversed it. Forts of Ali Masjid, Landi Kotal and some others were erected, from where armed levies operated under the overall command of the British viz, Mr Hastings, Colonel Warburton and Captain Barton. For sixteen years this arrangement worked well, and then the Afridis demanded the British to withdraw from Samana and Swat. They therefore rose to eliminate the forts near Khyber. The Orakazais also joined them, revolted at Kohat and attacked Samana.

That was where the iconic battle of Saragarhi came into play.

The Orakazais in a state of frustration for not having been able to fulfill their desire, turned for help to the Amir. They argued for Islam and resorted to *'Jihad'*. They submitted their total allegiance to the Amir and to fight under his instructions and management. They lauded their prowess of eliminating some forts except Samana. They requested for further help and guidance.

The Amir refused to meet the deputation. He sent a reply telling them that there were agreements among the parties. The British had violated none that was agreed upon. It was the tribesmen of the Frontiers who violated what was agreed upon. They had backed out and thus they must tend to their affairs by themselves into which the Amir would not like to be drawn.

Note: Letters from the Mullas and reply by the Amir are given in appendices enclosed later.

Lionel James writes: "*One is inclined to sum the causes of the outbreak under three heads the first of which is fanaticism; the second fanaticism; and the third fanaticism.*"

The Flash Point

Afghan patience transited to retaliation during the third and fourth weeks of August 1897. They captured and burnt forts of Khyber Pass, viz; Landi Kotal, Ali Masjid and Fort Maude. On 7th August, they burnt village Shankargarh and attacked Shabkadr. They were incited by the success of the Wazirs in Tochi Valley, fighting at Malakand and Shabkadr. On 28th August they destroyed the post at Shinwari, followed by firing at Hangu camp.

Aim of the Campaign

The aim of the campaign was to march through the country of Orakazais and Afridis, taking punitive action where required, and to announce from the heart of the country the final terms which will be imposed. Success would re-establish British prestige and ensure security from Russia.

The Force for Tirah Campaign

The Force was placed under the command of General Sir William Stephen Alexander Lockhart, KCB. The Main Column, the First Division, was under the command of Brigadier (local rank – Major General), William Penn Symons, CB. Its First Brigade was under Colonel S.M. Hamilton CB, DSO, later taken over by Brigadier General R.C. Hart, VC, CB. The Second Brigade was commanded by Brigadier General A. Gaselee, CB. The Second Division was commanded by Major General A.G. Yeatman-Biggs CB. The Third Brigade was commanded by Brigadier General (temporary Major

General) F.J. Kempster DSO and the Fourth by Brigadier General Westmacott CB DSO. The detailed composition of the Force is given in an Appendix later.

The Preparations

The intermittent attacks on the British establishments were unpalatable to the British. Numerous excursions undertaken had not achieved a lasting effect. They thus planned, once and for all, to teach a lesson to the tribesmen and subjugate them. It was known that the Afridis and Orakazais fighters totalled 40–50,000. It was Autumn, not suitable for a campaign by a large force. The best time was spring when the valleys of Maidan, Tirah, Mastura and Bara bloomed with resources. Thereafter, the severe winters would have prevented the tribesmen to move to and fro, giving ample time to the British to consolidate. But the British could not wait that long lest it was taken as their weakness. They decided to withstand the perils of weather conditions and strike without delay. A force of the finest regiments was placed under the command of General Sir William Lockhart.

It was expected that the tribesmen would be able to muster quite a substantial strength to fight at selected places of suitable defence since total concentration was not possible. The area was difficult, passes were few and the defiles were held by the tribesmen. They were known to be ferocious fighters, had formidable weapons, and were in a mood of religious frenzy. The British appreciated that the move would be on long lines of communications which were limited. 'The Tirah Expeditionary Force' that was assembled was of strength of almost 1010 British officers, 10,882 British troops, 491 native officers, 22,123 native troops, 197 hospital assistants, 179 clerks, 19,558 followers, 8000 horses, 18,384 mules and ponies and 1440 hospital riding ponies. Also there were camels, carts, and ponies which were utilized to improve lines of communication and assist logistic support.

The plan was resolved around the Tirah as its aim. It had never been penetrated, even visited by the British or any European. Two options were considered. The first option was to keep the entire force moving on one axis along the Dargai Heights – Sampagha Pass – Arhanga Pass and move to Maidan Valley. The other was to divide it into two columns, one moving along the first avenue and the second column from Kohat to Landukai Pass into Mastura Valley and then join up with the main body.

Finally, it was decided that the main force was to be kept intact and not divided into two as that might prove to be unsuccessful. It was essential strategically to have a strong force at the point of impact. Also, the inferior transport system had to be on one line and not divided. A column from Peshawar to Bara valley was analyzed. A mixed brigade 'Peshawar Column' was to operate from Peshawar as per requirement. Another mixed brigade was formed at Rawalpindi as a reserve. A force – 'Kurram Movable Column' was located at Hangu-Parachinar for employment as required. A mountain battery, two native regiments and four infantry battalions were tasked to hold the line of communication of the main column between Kohat and Tirah. Thus the Force was kept intact and the lure to move on different axis was rejected. Also, advantage was taken of the safe areas available up to Shinauri, which was in British territory. Unknown to the British, the Orakazais had collected at the Western edge of Samana range, from where they could observe the British preparations.

It would be of interest to note that all the Sikh units then formed a part of the Force. Punjab Frontier Force, 53rd Sikhs formed part of the Second Brigade, 15th (The Ludhiana Sikh) Regiment of Bengal Infantry Third Brigade of Second division, 36th (Sikh) Regiment of Bengal Infantry in Fourth Brigade and 45th (Rattray's Sikh) Regiment was part of the Peshawar Column. 35th Sikhs and 38th Dogras and others operated from Nowshera to reach Dargai on 29 July 1897.

An expedition on Tirah meant one against hard hitting Afridis and Orakazais who knew well that retribution would be forthcoming sooner or later for their acts of flouting the agreement and for capturing the British forts. On the other hand, the British were left with no other choice but to undertake an expedition to sort out the perpetual problem once and for all. They knew that they would be proceeding in a country un-reconnaitered, treacherous and of insurmountable terrain difficulties. They also knew that apart from the main forces of Afridis and Orakazais, they would have to deal with the Wazirs in Tochi Valley to the South, the Mohmands, the Barauris and Swats in the North.

The Execution: Dargai Heights – Khanki Valley

On 18 October, the Second Division under Major General Yeatman Biggs advanced to dislodge the tribesmen from Village Dargai and the ridges close by, to secure them for subsequent operations on the only road to

Khanki Valley. Geographically, it was hostile country, deep ravines and numerous heights that were formidable to negotiate. The lines of communication were poor. Dargai is located on a cliff at a height of 6000 feet and is a tough nut to crack. Shelling on the positions did not have much effect. The tribesmen had taken to the natural cover of rocks where they had built 'sangars' and walls. The 4th Brigade under General Westmacott attacked the positions while the 3rd Brigade under General Kempster outflanked with Gordon Highlanders and 45th Sikhs. The 36th Sikhs was deployed at Samana Suk to provide protection to the right flank of the attack. Meanwhile, several thousand Afridis joined the fray from Khanki Valley. The assault by the 2nd Gurkhas, followed by Gordon Highlanders, had achieved substantial success but was abandoned due to stiff resistance and added reasons of scarcity of water, food and warm clothing. The Force Commander felt that keeping the Dargai Heights occupied would give away surprise as it would reveal the intended route. However, this decision did not find acceptability as later when the move was resumed the Heights were found to be occupied. After two days, on 20th October, two brigades again were employed and after a stiff fight captured Dargai Height, suffering many casualties. Gordon Highlanders, 2nd Gurkhas, 15th Sikhs, 2nd Battalion the Derbyshire Regiment and Ist battalion the Dorseshire Regiment participated in this spectacular attack. Number 8 and 9 Mountain Batteries assisted.

'To Colonel Haughton and his men, burning as they must have been to avenge the butchery at Saragarhi, such inaction would be hard to bear.'

It was an extremely cold night and the troops descended in the morning to the Khanki Valley. Though there was no enemy confronted, the move was on a goat track that engineers had to improve at every step. 36th Sikhs were the rearguard and had an extremely tough time since they had to tender to the baggage being carried on wayward donkeys, jumping, slipping and scrambling. The loads slipped and had to be secured again, causing delay. The chained mules and donkeys created havoc as wrong action by one meant two or three or all skidding, pulled forward, or held back or all falling. The rearguard responsibility also meant tremendous alertness against the sniping or raiding enemy parties. The unit along with Northamptons moved to Shinaura, a 12 miles distance in difficult country.

Here at Karappa and Khangarbar in the Khanki valley, a week was spent by the Force reorganizing itself and reconnoitering for further move.

The tribesmen kept up sniping, firing a volley when they found Britishers on the crest line, thus causing steady attrition.

Short of the Sampagha Pass is the village of Gadki, along which was found a convenient position for deployment of artillery. The suitable approach to attack was a long spur, with a depression in-between. On top was a round knoll which concealed the *'sangars'* made by the tribesmen.

Khanki Valley and Sampagha Pass

1st and 2nd Divisions had camped 6-7 miles short of Sampagha Pass and closed by 27th October. There was delay on the part of the British which gave time to the tribesmen to reinforce the Pass to a strength of 10,000 to 12,000. For five-six days, skirmishes occurred including artillery barrages. A few personnel of 5th Gurkhas and 15th Sikhs were wounded, including an officer of each unit. The presence of Sir William Lockhart at the most crucial junctures always clinched the issue, and the same thing was repeated here. On 27th October, 36th Sikhs and Northamptons were ordered to climb the hills on the right. On the left, the Yorks, 45th Sikhs and Gurkhas marched up. Lockhart was himself in the main body of the 1st Division. On 29th October, the Pass was attacked, and heavily bombarded by artillery. 36th Sikh was also part of the attacking force along with the Yorkshires. The climb was almost perpendicular. The King's Own Scottish Borders provided fire support. The Sikhs captured the third and final position against stiff opposition. The momentum of attack was at its best to capture the Pass at the height of 6700 feet. The Pathans did not give a pitched battle as was expected and vanished when pressurized by artillery fire and the upcoming attack. According to Colonel Haughton, 36th Sikhs were the first to cross Sampagha on 30th October. The Mastura Valley could be seen from there, at its sublime best – green fields, blooming crops and well built houses. The Orakazais had fled to the hills and beyond leaving behind enormous amounts of food and useful items.

Arhanga Pass

From Mastura Valley, Arhanga was five miles away. It leads into Tirah proper. On 30th October, reconnaissance of the Pass was undertaken. The plans to capture it were hashed. A suitable position for deployment of artillery was found. It was estimated to be defended by 1000 Afghans.

Geographically, the area suited the attacker since it was less broken, was wrest of ravines and provided space for turning movements. However, it was felt that shelters and *'sangars'* behind the rocks might render artillery fire ineffective. It was also felt that the Afridis would fight to the hilt to stop the British ingress into their precious Tirah.

2nd Division was to lead, the advance guard being the 4th Brigade, followed by the 3rd Brigade. The advantage of plunging fire by the enemy was made use of. The Yorkshire Regiment, 5th Gurkhas, 45th Sikhs, and 4th Gurkhas moved forward admirably. To the good luck of the British, the Pathans did not give a fight and melted into the hills. The units were quickly moved into Tirah Maidan. The Afridis got their families together and ran for their lives. Captain Searle of 36th Sikhs and some soldiers were wounded in these operations. The Mastura Valley, Maidan and Rajgul were soon invested. It was noticed that there were many good houses where the Afridis lived. There were also escape places in the hills where they shifted in summers or when forced out from the Valley.

There were skirmishes with the most ferocious clans, the Zakka Khel of Afridis, especially on 31st October and 1st November. The Pathans swooped down from the crags and carried off rifles, ammunition and baggage of many units including the Royal West Surrey Regiment, 15th and 45th Sikhs. It affected their morale. However, the British did overcome the problem and asked for the *'Jirgahs'* to surrender. The tribesmen had suffered and appreciated the British determination to push forward. They also realized they could not fight with the British in the open since the latter were well organized, kept lines of communication open and camps well secured.

Life at Tirah was unpleasant as Afidis kept up reprisals. The troops were happy advancing or fighting as that presented achievements. But pause was necessary because of political considerations for negotiations. Yet it was felt *'you cannot make omelets without breaking eggs, and you cannot make war with kid gloves'*. The Afghans however could not understand why the British halted. They continued with their activities of harassment.

But it was also a fact that the tribesmen were in need of food grains that they had buried earlier. To forestall this effort the Britishers launched an operation on 09 November 1897 to Saransar in the Zakka Khel country.

Bagh

The drainage lines from the oval Maidan basin converge at Bagh cutting deep into slopes of the foothills. The sides of these waterways are precipitous and not negotiable. On the sides, there were terraced steps used for cultivation.

At this stage, it was felt that the Afridis had been punished adequately. The tribes had been turned into fugitives whose survival was to make do in the bitter cold hills. They were in awe of the British resolve to advance further. The Force had camped in the beautiful valleys of pure water, green forests and groves.

Saransar

Saransar is 8000 feet high. It was about five miles from where the British were camping. The road over it led from Maidan to Bara Valley. The troops under Brigadier General Westmacott took on the expedition to capture Saransar on 09 November 1897. 36th Sikhs assisted Northamptons to pass through and to carry out their task towards Saransar, yet on their way they had far too many casualties. It was also a tedious task for 36th Sikhs to keep the route safe. 15th Sikhs were guarding the right flank. Artillery took up positions on a hill on the right. The Northamptons got entrapped by the Pashtuns. Lieutenant Van Someren of the 36th took upon himself to help them and in the process got wounded along with some of his men. 15th suffered some casualties in a hand to hand fight. Northamptons were extricated from a very precarious plight.

The Zakkha Khels were active throughout resorting to guerilla tactics, ambushing, sniping and finally attacking in force wherever feasible.

While at Tirah, a number of moves on the surrounding hills were carried out on 12th November, bringing sense to the Pathans. The older people desired negotiations, but the younger defied their authority, though at heart wanting to settle matters to their advantage. The Orakazai *'Jirgahs'* were called upon by Lockhart, who gave his terms clearly as:

(a) Full restoration of all arms and property etc looted from Khyber forts or subsequently.

(b) Surrender of 500 breach loading rifles.

(c) Payment of a fine of Rs 30,000.

(d) Forfeit of all subsidies and advances granted to the tribesmen in the past.

(e) Formal submission to be tendered.

The *'Jirgas'* were given time up to 26 November to decide. The attention meanwhile was diverted to Afridi *'Jirgas'*.

Tseri Kandao Pass: Waran Valley

'Tseri' means 'Oak free Pass' and *'Kandao'* means 'Top of the Pass'. On 13th November, Brigadier General Kempster was sent to the Waran Valley to realize whether the Afridis had understood the terms to follow in future. The route was through Tseri Kandao Pass. The Force had Dorsets, 15th and 36th Sikhs, 2nd Gurkhas, 8 Mountain Battery and sappers. For the next two days the Force carried out its mission successfully by hard hitting operations. The House of Mulla Sayid Akbar was destroyed. His pulpit was captured as a memento. However, the mosque attached to the house was spared. 2nd Gurkhas, 3rd Gurkha Scouts and Gordons displayed vigour, chivalry and achievement. In one of the houses, a quoit which is worn by the Sikhs over their turban and can be used to throw as a weapon on an enemy, with blood soaked hair was found, perhaps an appalling act of the Pathans on one of the soldiers of Saragarhi.

15th and 36th Sikhs were detailed to hold Tseri Kandao Pass.

While the Force was returning on 16th November, the Afridis moved down from heights of Saransar and surrounded 15th Sikhs, who fought resolutely. The 36th who had moved out from their positions, had to retract their steps along with Dorsets to support the 15th. Dorsets suffered numerous casualties including 11 officers; so fierce was the battle. The Afridis engaged them in hordes. The situation was thus, the 15th trying to get back while half of 36th Sikh was endeavouring to join them. One of the officers, Captain Lawrence of 15th Sikhs had been shot dead while two of 36th Sikhs Captain Custance and Lieutenant Munn were wounded. It was getting dark, the hills were precipitous, and the enemy was amassed all around. The Dorsets were also against a formidable foe. Ammunition with the British was low while the Afridis had plenty. All the four battalions of the Brigade had suffered casualties. However, they made it to the camp carrying their dead and wounded. The 36th fought for some houses where they took refuge. Both the columns, under the Commanding Officer and Second in Command, displayed utmost bravery and praise from all.

Bagh and Dwatoi (the two rivers)

After rest and recoup for three days, the Force moved to Bagh on 18th November. There were numerous houses, each prepared as a fortress. Sir William Lockhart ordered all these to be destroyed, perhaps not in anger, but as instinct of self preservation. He also addressed 15th Sikhs and praised them for their gallant actions. On 21st, *'Jirgas'* of four clans were dictated terms as follows:

(a) Restoration of all arms and property etc plundered at Khyber forts and at other occasions.

(b) Surrender of 800 breach loading rifles.

(c) Payment of Rs 50,000 as a fine.

(d) Formal tender of submission in an open Darbar.

(e) That the Government reserved the right to decide hereafter the question of management and administration of Khyber Pass.

Dwatoi

Orders were then given to Brigadier General Westmacott to march from Bagh to Dwatoi to punish Kuki Khel. The Force constituted of 28th Bombay Pioneers, King's Own Scottish Borderers, 3rd Gurkhas, 36th Sikhs, No 4 Company Madras Sappers, No 3 Company Bombay Sappers, the Gurkha Scouts and No 5 Mountain Battery. Both sides of the defile were cleared by the Yorks and 2nd Gurkhas. A seven mile long road along a cold stream had to be negotiated. The road ran almost through the stream. The Force was in dire straits since it was terribly windy and cold through the Dwatoi defile. 36th Sikh did a splendid job as rearguard, fighting the tribesmen and suffering some casualties in the process. It had taken two days to the move to Dwatoi, one day there and one day to return. 23rd at Dwatoi was utilized to reconnoiter in various directions. On 24th, the move back to Bagh started. It was again 36th Sikhs who was rearguard and escorted baggage on the wayward mules. The Force had done quite a successful excursion. At this stage there were rumours that the political leaders were averse to a continued struggle. There was dilly dallying in furthering the operations. A chance was given to the Afridis to surrender.

The withdrawal of the Force which had been quite successful in accomplishing its aim was indicated, duly prompted by the foul weather, which had turned from bad to worse. It rained heavily. Sleet and snow further hampered the move. Carrying the wounded in *'dhoolis'* was extremely cumbersome. The tribesmen kept up their harassing tactics. At places it seemed there was a rout rather than a planned withdrawal.

The Correspondent of 'Times of India', wrote: *"It was a most masterly retirement, and the whole Force is enthusiastic over General Westmacott's handling of his small forces, and of magnificent work of Colonel Haughton and the 36th Sikhs. This is the fifth rearguard action which they have been called upon to fight during the last month and on each occasion they have acquitted themselves like men. Six officers have been wounded, and considerably over a hundred men killed or wounded, since the first attack was made on the Samana Range. The reconnaissance to Dwatoi from Tirah Maidan deserves the historical, not only on account of hardships which the men cheerily endured, but on account of the magnificent way both the advancement and retirement were conducted, the gorge being the worst that any frontier soldier has seen in the Frontier wars."*

Move to Bara and Waran Valleys

The 3rd and 4th Brigades leaped forward. On 10th December 1997, started the arduous march to the Bara Valley. 36th Sikhs were detailed as the advance guard. Excerpts of a letter by Colonel Haughton written on 09 December from Dwatoi is enclosed as appendix.

The 1st Brigade carried out operations in the Mastura Valley against the Orakazais who were not as hostile and ferocious as the Afridis in Tirah. There were some skirmishes in which the British along with the natives battered the Pathans. The 1st Gurkhas carried out highly praiseworthy operations against the Chamkanis at the Northern end of the Kurram Valley. The Massarais were surprised, their *'jirga'* tendering submission. Some Malliks were killed in the Kurram Valley. The Peshawar Column advanced to Barkai via Dwatoi on 8th December, thus the entire area including Jamrud, Bara and Bazar Valley, up to Khyber Pass was visited. By 28th December, the Force had crossed the Passes and concentrated at Dargai.

The move back via the Dwatoi defile was undertaken. The Brigades leaped forward. By 9th December, Maidan had been evacuated and on 10th, the advance to Bara Valley was started. It was tough going from Dwatoi to Sandana, Sherkhel, Naokandai, to Sawaikot – a total of 34 miles. A number of military actions had to be undertaken. The Afridis had Martini-Henry rifles, having a range of 1200 to 1500 yards. They also had some Lee-Metfords. The maximum brunt fell upon 36th Sikh which was on rearguard duty along with the 3rd Gurkhas. They performed outstandingly.

The whole Force, reached Sawaikot, and the first phase of the campaign ended here. The 2nd Division was rested at Bara-Barkai, having withstood all the hard fighting. The 1st Division concentrated at Jamrud.

Bazar Valley, Khyber and Shinkamar

The Peshawar Column returned to Jamrud from Sawaikot and joined the 1st Division on 19th. On the 25th, the Division reached Bazar Valley. The Force further marched to Lala, China, near Ali Masjid and destroyed its towers and defences after some skirmishes enroute. Brigadier General Hart's Brigade marched to Karamna and Burg. The Afridis kept up their harassment of the Force. The Brigade returned to Jamrud on 30th December. While the above operations were being executed, General Hemmond's Column reached Landi Kotal on 26th December. Thereafter, the repairs of the forts and roads were undertaken earnestly.

At the same time, the 2nd Division which had rested at Mamanai and Bara, was ordered to explore the remaining areas. On 28th December 1898, the 4th Brigade which was at Mamanai was ordered towards the Shinkamar Pass and told to occupy the Kotal by 10 am on 29 December. The secret was somehow let out and the Afridis came to know of the move. The Mamanai's Column King's own Yorkshire Light Infantry, 200 rifles of 36th Sikhs in four Companies under Colonel Haughton and two guns of No 5 (Bombay) attacked boldly. Due to a communication error, a company of 36th Sikh was prematurely withdrawn from a commanding position along the Shinkamar Pass. The Afridis took advantage and seized it. Yorkshires in order to capture the vacated position pressed in three companies who had some success but were found to be overlooked from another ridge from where accurate fire was brought upon them.

Haughton sent three companies down the Pass and remained on the hill with one company to cover the Yorkshire's retreat. The 36th Sikhs Adjutant Lieutenant Turning was with the CO. Yorkshires could not retire because of stiff opposition which Colonel Haughton and his company engaged fiercely. Haughton and Turning fought gallantly and were martyred there. Haughton had picked up a rifle from a Yorkshire wounded soldier. He was with about six men and fully engaged with the Pathans at a short distance, when he was hit in the head and died a brave man, leading from the front. His death was lamented deeply by all because he had become famous owing to his courage, cool demeanour, striking judgment and resourceful execution

Sir Wlliam Lockhart said about Colonel Haughton, "*With his determination, strategic and tactical shrewdness, a pushing posture yet a remarkable humbleness had won over the hearts of his command as well as the Afridis*".

More on Haughton in the following chapter.

Owing to the events from January to March, the Afridis realized they could not last long against the British, particularly since the winters were getting over and they apprehended another expedition by the Britishers. Sir William Lockhart convinced them of their futility of continuing the struggle. The Tirah Campaign had achieved its aim and therefore the Force was reduced to one Division to control some of the most difficult areas ever penetrated by any force as such.

Casualties

A summary of casualties of the Tirah Campaign, from 12th October till 6th April 1898 are as under:

Killed, all ranks	287
Wounded	853
Missing	10
Total	1150

Officers: British killed 23, wounded 56

Indian killed 04, wounded 16.

Note: Names of above personnel omitted since records are not available.

Casualties 36th Sikhs

Samana – Killed BOs–1, wounded 1; Indian officer wounded 1; OR killed 21, wounded 45.

Tirah – Killed BOs–2, wounded 7; ORs killed 15, wounded 57.

About the medical services rendered during the campaign, Hutchison wrote: "*Amid the clash of arms, the hum of the camps, the commotion of marches and the turmoil of retreats, the great Military Medical Services, British and Indian, are apt to receive scant notice from the chronicles of events, ...*".

Awards 36th Sikhs

During the complete operation, 36th Sikhs earned the following awards:

• Distinguished Service Order (DSO)	02
• To Brevet Colonel	01
• To Brevet Major	01
• Indian Order of Merit (IOM)	54 (*A record in itself*)
• Mentioned in Despatches	38
• One murraba (25 acres) of land to each	30 (Plus a reward of Rs 300

Battle Honour: Saragarhi was granted as a Battle Honour for the Regiment. In March 1900, a G.G.O. (No 16) was issued authorizing the Regiment to bear upon the Colours and honorary distinctions specified below in commemoration of the gallant conduct and distinguished service during the operations on the North-West Frontier of India in 1997-88:

(a) Punjab Frontier.

(b) Samana.

(c) Tirah.

Conclusion

The fact remains that both sides had exhausted themselves, both did not want to continue operations, yet both sides asserted that they had won the day. The campaign was one of the most difficult with mixed results. The Pathans proved that it was not only a *'jihad'* as such for them to unite all and fight for their religion, but also inspired them to throw away the perpetrators of usurpation of their lands and customs. The Britishers concluded, at least most of them, that the campaigns and expeditions were not to subjugate people but a political necessity to establish superiority of the British.

The plaintive tone of Queen Victoria's letter to the Viceroy of India shows her angst very clearly, *"As we did not wish to retain any part of the country, is the continuation and indefinite prolongation of these punitive expeditions really justifiable at the cost of many valuable lives?"*

THE TIRAH CAMPAIGN 1897-98
BRITISH EXPEDITIONARY FORCE AND EXECUTION

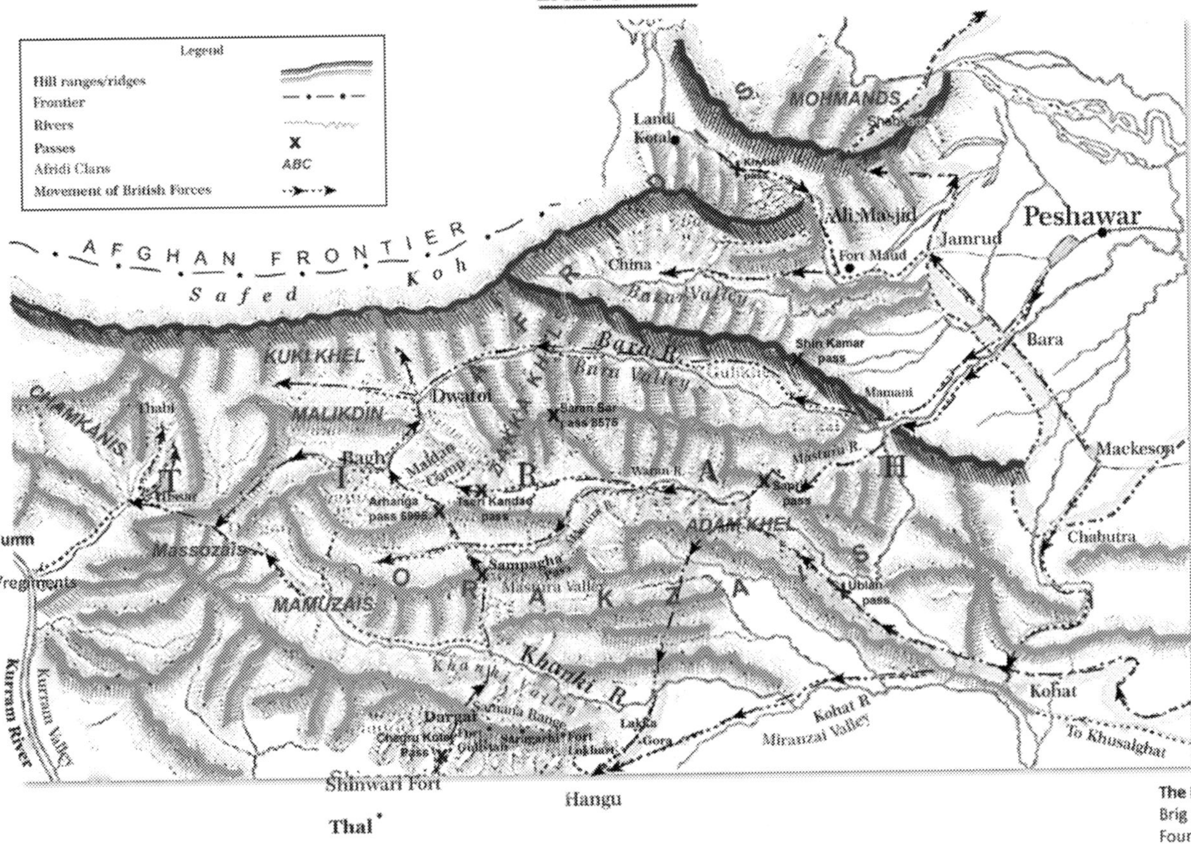

The Kurram Movable Column
Col W Hill
Three infantry battalions/regiments
Two cavalry regiments
One field battery

The Peshawar Column
Brig Gen AG Hamod CB, DSO, VC, ADC
Four infantry units
Two field/mountain batteries
One regiment cavalry
Sappers and Miners units

The Rawal Pindi Reserve
Brig Gen CR Macgregor, DSO
Four infantry battalions
Jodhpur Lancers

The Main Column

First Division – Brig Gen WP Symons, CB

First Brigade – Brig Gen RC Hart, VC, CB
Four battalions
Second Brigade – Brig Gen A Gaselee, CB
Four battalions
Divisional Troops
Three mountain batteries
Two squadrons cavalry
Pioneers, Sappers and Miners
Nabha infantry battalion

Second Division
Maj Gen G Yeatman-Biggs, CB

Third Brigade – Col FJ Kempster DSO, ADC
Four infantry battalions
Fourth Brigade – Brig Gen R Westmacot CB, DSO
Four infantry battalions
Divisional Troops
Three mountain batteries
Two cavalry squadrons
Pioneers, sappers and Miners
Jhind Infantry battalion

Line of communications
Lt Gen Sir AP Palmer, KCB
Four infantry battalions/regiments
One mountain battery
Two regiments cavalry
Sappers and miners
Hospitals, Transport, Ordnance depots and Engineer units.

Key Officers
Supreme Political Power and Military Control – Sir William Lockhart
Adjutant general and Chief of Staff – Brig Gen WG Nicholson, CB
Commanding Royal Artillery – Brig Gen CH Spragge
Commanding Engineers – Brig Gen JE Broadbent
Principal medical Officer – Surgeon Colonel (Temporary Rank Maj Gen) Thomson CB
The Political Officers – Sir Richard Udny, KCSI and Col Warburton, CSI
Messers King, Hastings, Donald, Blakeway

Note: Adequate medical staff, equipment and medicines provided with each formation

Excerpts from a letter written by Colonel Haughton to General Sir Charles Gough, give his impressions lucidly about the Tirah Expedition, something which he had seen and endured himself, are given in an Appendix H.

The campaign terminated on 03 April 1898.

EMINENT PERSONALITIES

Abdur Rahman Khan
Amir of Afghanistan
(1880-1901

Sir Henry Mortimer Durand
Diplomat and Civil servant
of Colonial India

Sir WM. Lockhart
(Supreme political power
and military control)

Major-General Sir William Penn Symons
KCB (First Division)

Maj Gen G Yeatman-Biggs, CB
(Second Division)

TIRAH CAMPAIGN

The Kohat Pass

Shinwari Camp

Assault at Sampagha Pass

Arrangha Pass Summit

Dargai Cliffs

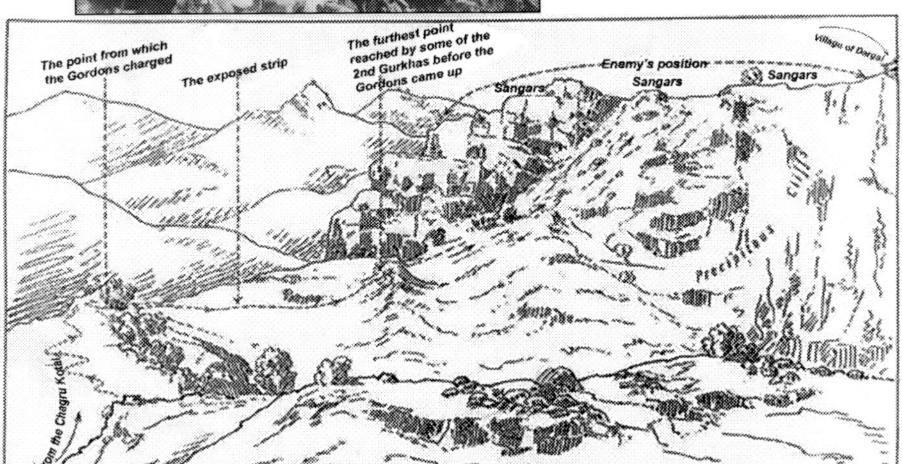

Sketch showing Attack to capture Dargai Height

TIRAH CAMPAIGN

Maidan Camp

Dawatoi Defile

Mosque at Bagh

Dictating terms to Jirgah at Peshawar

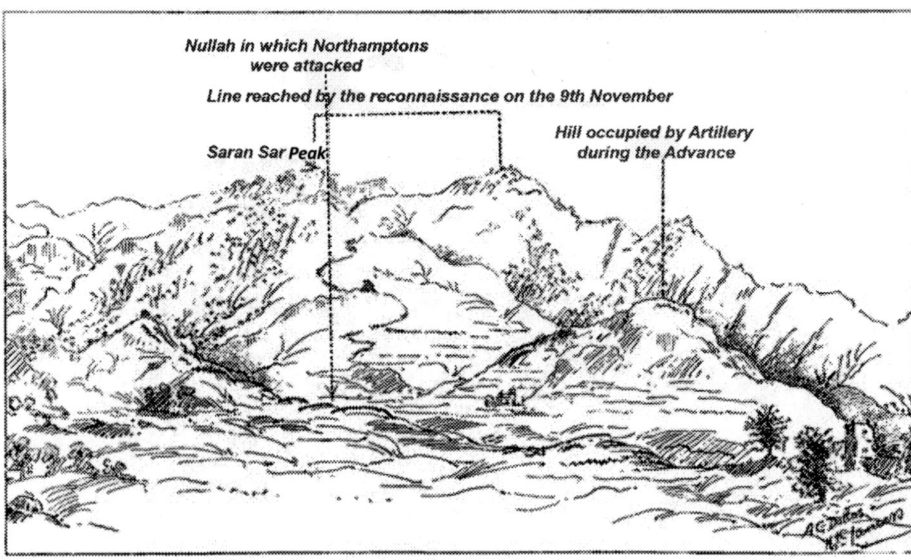

Attack at Saransar

TIRAH CAMPAIGN

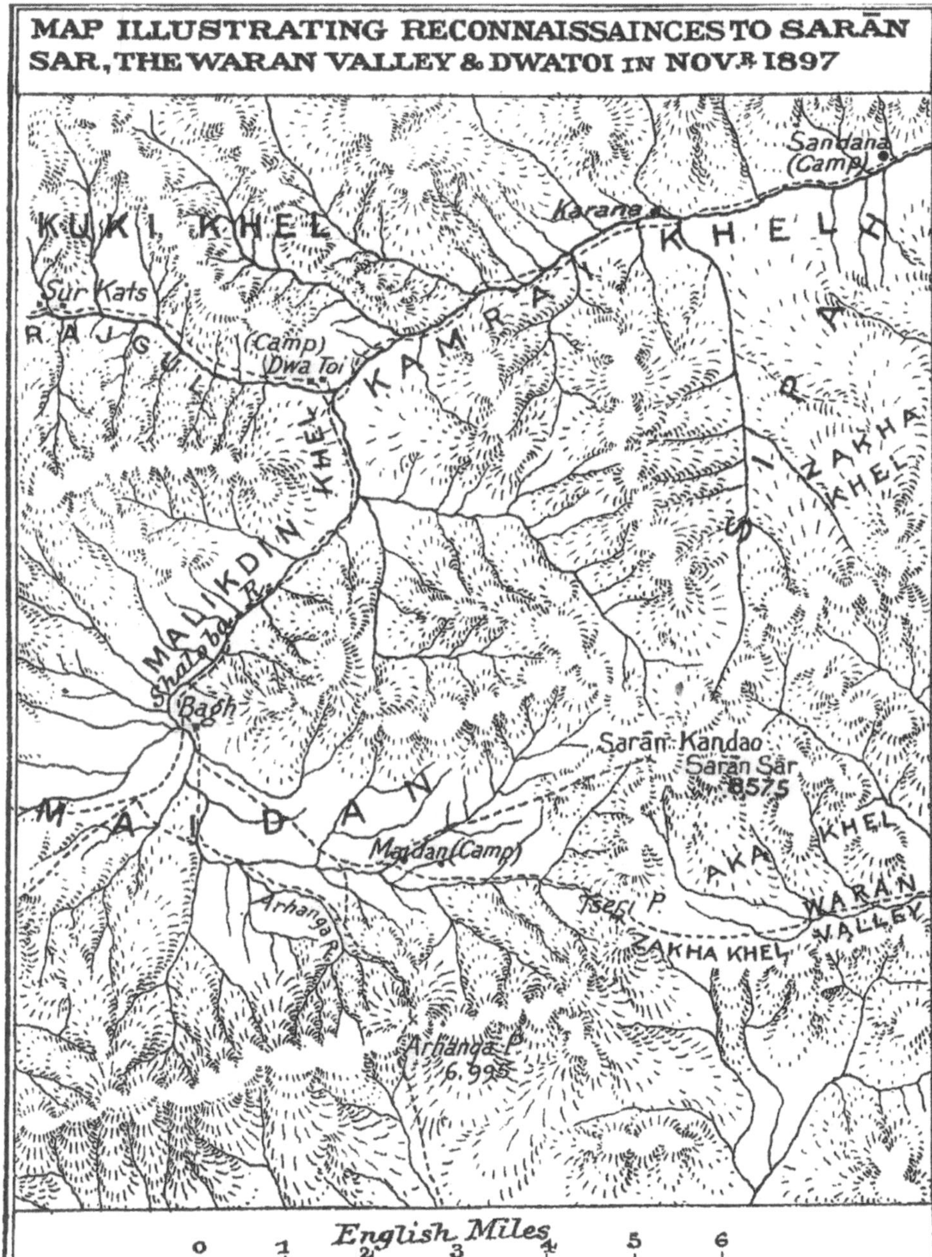

Saransar, Waran and Dwatoi

CHAPTER EIGHT

LIEUTENANT COLONEL JOHN HAUGHTON

> *"A hero is someone who has given his or her life to something bigger than oneself."*
>
> – Joseph Campbell

It is axiomatic that when the men fought so gallantly, there had to be something tangible besides training and discipline, that reminded and goaded them on, inculcating a spirit of extreme bravery and sacrifice, an extraordinary strength of mind to accomplish what was ordered and what was expected. What Havildar Ishar Singh was to a band of twenty one (including a noncombatant) under his command, the same were the commanders in the chain, specially the Commanding Officer, Lieutenant Colonel John Haughton. What he was, what he did, how he conducted himself and how he treated his command to follow him to the last, what would have been the most binding and inspiring traits of his personality. He was a leader who demonstrated how he developed and performed. It would be essential to have a peep into his childhood, adolescence and grooming as an officer, in command of a unit so magnificently during a period of tussle and violence, against a redoubtable foe, under most trying conditions in the area of operations, and ultimately when the time came, to die so exemplary well.

It is an established fact that Junior Commissioned Officers (JCOs) and a Non Commissioned Officers (NCOs), especially the latter, are the backbone of a unit. Then it is the CO who nurtures and stiffens that backbone. It is normal to plan a line of officers who are likely to take over command. It did not, however, work out in the case of Haughton who served in other units before he was found fit to be entrusted with the command of 36th Sikhs.

John or Jack, as popularly known, was born on 22 August 1852, at Chhota Nagpur, India, as the son of General Jack Calhoys Haughton. Both father and son had studied in the same school. John not only inherited the height and physique of his father but also his devotion to cause. General Haughton had displayed the finest soldierly qualities and a great sense of bravery, in spite of being wounded, as a Lieutenant, in 1841 defending Charikar, a strategically important place, forty miles North of Kabul. The same qualities were displayed by the son Lieutenant Colonel Haughton at Tirah – a grand case of hereditary courage.

Major A C Yates writes: *"The courage of a Haughton was instinctive. The defence of Charikar by the young subaltern of twenty four was a test of bravery and endurance with which no momentary flash of daring can compare; while the memory of John Haughton at Tseri Kandao, at Dwatoi, and at Shinkamar, will be handed down as a tradition of cool courage and steadfast valour. Neither father nor son, however, was decorated with the Victoria Cross."*

"The record of Tirah Expedition is the record of any army which most manfully performed the arduous task apportioned to it; and conspicuous among all his comrades in that expedition, in courage and moral grandeur as well as in inches, 'primus inter pares', stands forth – Lieutenant Colonel John Haughton of the 36th Sikhs, a soldier 'sans et sans reproche'".

General J C Haughton was wounded thrice in his career. It was said about him 'great ability, firmness and justice combined with high minded gentleness which won the hearts of all, Indians and Europeans'.

Lieutenant John Haughton was six and a half feet tall. His brother officer in 10th Bengal Infantry, Colonl C H Palmer wrote in 1887, *"At Jalpaiguri, one morning, Haughton was found in white uniform at distance away, when someone remarked, 'Why, here's Kinchanjunga got loose'" (snow clad mountain of 28,000 feet height).*

He had a lineage from famous families, both paternal and maternal. His paternal ancestors were highly educated and eminent people. They had settled down in Lancashire. John had two brothers, one studied medicine but joined the Civil Service in Assam and Bengal. Thereafter he switched to a tea planter's life, where he did a marvelous service. John's other brother, like him, joined the army and served during the Afghan campaign. John's mother was the daughter of a Colonel and sister of a Captain. Thus soldierly blood flowed in John's veins. His father in law had spent forty years in India. He was a man of versatile abilities, particularly remembered for his engineering feats.

John's childhood was mostly with his grandparents as his parents were in the field. He lived in Ramsgate, England, along with his brother and sister. He was known to be kind-hearted and amenable also resolute and independent. His teachers said he *'looked strong and valiant, a man to be depended on and trusted'*.

Haughton was fond of maintaining a diary and wrote numerous letters to his father, wife and others. They not only record the incidents of that time but also give an insight into his character. He passed out from the Royal College of Sandhurst and joined the South Wales Borderers, on 28 October 1871, at Gibraltar. He was transferred to the 72nd Highlanders at Peshawar. Thereafter he was posted as a staff officer to 10th Bengal Infantry at Dacca on 10 November 1876. This took him away from his father, though he maintained a steady stream of letters, a preserve of the family. He learnt Hindustani which enabled him to understand the Indian troops.

Haughton was married on 18 January 1883, at Barrackpore, to Margaretta Louisa Baker who died the next year. They had a son who was then brought up by the maternal grandmother. Haughton was in grief, but since he was fond of reading, got more engrossed to the study of the military profession.

In a letter written from Banda, dated October 24, 1885, he wrote to his father that the British Indian Army was going to be reorganized into regiments of three battalions each. A number of regiments were going to be raised. He expressed his wish to join one of the battalions of the new Sikh Regiment.

Though he had not done Staff College, yet he was posted as Brigade Major of the 1st Brigade, 2nd Division of Northern Force. To be identified with the job, in his own words, he said, *"I shall have to study the ways of our native regiments, and picking up hints and wrinkles there from."* His performance as a staff officer and understanding of field work was outstanding.

In June 1886, he was appointed to the 39th Bengal Infantry. However in March 1887, he learnt that the 10th Bengal Infantry was moving to Burma for active service, he resigned from the 39th in an effort to join the 10th. Instead, he was moved to 35th Sikhs, under raising along with 36th Sikhs, both comprising Jat Sikhs. He started studying the Punjabi dialect and history of the Sikhs. In September, he learnt about the death of his father and he went to England. On his return, he was appointed a wing commander in the 35th Sikhs as a Major. On 25 June 1894, he was bestowed with the command of 36th Sikhs, with a service of 24 years, which was considered an unusually early age.

He remarried at Durham to a Miss Helen Barmby on 18 September 1894. He along with his wife joined the 36th Sikhs at Ambala.

He marched with the unit to Bannu, where they stayed for five months. Then they moved to Peshawar where they stayed for one year and eight months. He was promoted to Lieutenant Colonel in November 1895. In December 1896, the unit moved to Kohat. In February 1897, they took over responsibility at Samana Ridge. His wife moved along with him and stayed at Fort Lockhart till May 1897, then returned to England. He was also well versed with 'Pushto'. He learnt camp life the hard way, by putting himself upfront always. He was firm but not aggressive, never 'wobbled', straight forward, genuine and true.

In the Frontier, he did a splendid job as Commanding Officer, on his first assignment at Samana. The unit was split in two wings. The left one under Captain D Gordon, arrived at Parchinar on 08 January 1897, with detachments at Thal and Sadda. The right wing was at Samana. The battles fought by troops under command of Haughton at Samana have already been described in Chapter Six. Here it would be appropriate to explain his efforts to assist others in distress and difficulty. When on 27 August, Fort Gulistan was surrounded and attacked by thousands of tribesmen, he personally led a force of one officer and 130 other ranks from Fort Lockhart to assist. He responded to the situation by moving half the force to Fort Lockhart when he learnt it was being besieged. On 28th, learning that Gogra and Tsalai had been captured, the levies and border police having given no fight to the attackers, he moved back to Lockhart to ensure its defence. Responding to a military situation, he immediately took remarkably correct decisions with flexibility and resource fulness and thus turning the tables on the adversary.

On 03 September, when he learnt that a large force had assembled opposite Gulistan, he once again personally led reinforcements there. The troops at Gulistan had fought gallantly. The Orakazais were defeated and they vanished from the field. Satisfied, Haughton returned to Lockhart. But hardly had he done that, when swarms of Orakazais again assembled around Gulistan and a firing duel ensued between the two.

When Saragarhi was under severe attack, he conveyed to his men to conserve ammunition. He had assessed accurately how much his men had fired and how much was left with them to fight an intriguing battle. He was observing the ensuing battle continuously, and fully aware of the logistics, in full control of developing situations and thus responded as an outstanding leader.

In the afternoon of the attack on Saragarhi, the Afghans had affected a breach in the fort at a dead angle. It should be appreciated how much concern and anxiety a Commanding Officer would have undergone realizing the gravity of the situation that prevailed at that time. He could not hold himself, and once again rose to the occasion. With Lieutenant Munn and some men they ventured out of the fort positioning themselves at a distance of about 100 yards from the attackers, and then engaged them to divert their attention. He was all the time watchful to keep his route back to Lock Hart under observation and safe lest he be cut off by the Pathans who were threatening from all around. His efforts showed a resolve not to let his men fall unaided. Yet when he reached Saragarhi, he found hundreds of Pathans around and inside the post, and thus all was over.

On the 13th, a force under General Yeatman Biggs approached Sangar and Fort Lockhart. Meanwhile the tribesmen had started withdrawing. Colonel Haughton took it on himself and sallied forward engaging the enemy.

How Colonel Haughton perceived the grim situation, what he felt about the gallant actions of his brave men and his personal responses are best narrated by him in his letters to his wife dated 13, 15 and 16 September 1897, given in Appendix D.

Thereafter, peace and respite in the battle was best utilized by the troops in rest, training, recuperation and preparation logistically for a campaign to be launched in which 36th Sikhs under Haughton performed brilliantly.

When the 3rd Brigade attacked to capture Dargai Heights, 36th Sikhs along with the Northampton Regiment was tasked to move to Talai Spur to provide protection from that direction to the assaulting Brigade. In a letter Haughton showed his angst having been denied an opportunity to attack Dargai Heights and take revenge against those who had attacked Saragarhi.

During a further move, 36th Sikhs performed all tasks of picqueting and foraging efficiently under the spectacular command of Haughton. He led the unit from the front capturing the Afghan's second and third positions at Sampagha Pass. His planning and execution were most praiseworthy at Saran Sar and Tseri Kandao. His guidance to have proper reconnaissance of the tough country, precipitous deep ravines, steep cliffs, appreciation of terrible winds and sound tactical approach paid rich dividends during several tasks entrusted to his unit, achieving success with least casualties. His quick grasp of the situation and action taken saved many a situations viz; helping 15th Sikhs to get out of a precarious situation in Waren Valley. The camaraderie of both the units was at its best and the initiative taken by Haughton on his own paid good dividends. Against their own marginal casualties, the enemy suffered almost three hundred dead. All felt that, "The officer in command had shown not only courage but presence of mind, endurance and resource. Moreover, he had acted on his own initiative and responsibility."

On the move of the Brigade to Dwatoi, Haughton was given the rearguard responsibility again. The distance to be covered was only six miles, but the move through a narrow defile and Afghans' continuous relentless onslaught was arduous. The responsibility of safeguarding the baggage also fell on 36th Sikh, a very cumbersome job against the enemies Lee-Metford rifles. The unit however returned to Bagh. The responsibility was carried out with aplomb for which Haughton was highly praised.

The strain of the last three months was too much even for a stout soldier like Haughton, he fell sick and was off duty for a few days. However, his resilience was supreme and on getting well he rejoined duty.

The Force to occupy the Shinkamar Pass included 200 rifles of 36th Sikh, under Lieutenant Colonel Haughton, who formed the advance guard. They were then ordered to cross over the Kotal to help the Yorkshires who were in a difficult situation. Haughton, along with Lieutenant Turning, his Adjutant, two Sikhs and two men of Yorkshires were surrounded by the enemy who were a few yards from them. In the melee, Haughton in an effort to help Yorkshires, took a Lee-Metford rifle from a wounded Yorkshire man and engaged the enemy. He was advised by a fellow soldier not to expose himself, but he was fearless and refused to take cover as he felt he was the best facing the enemy when right in front. Haughton instructed the Yorks to fix bayonets, and said, "We'll shoot away all the ammunition we've got, and then show them how British soldiers die." As fate would have it, he was hit in the head by an enemy bullet; he fell and died instantaneously, fortunate to have died nobly, endeavouring to save others.

One Yorkshire man who was lucky to survive told the story of end of a most fabulous man.

Major A C Yate wrote: "*If there was one guiding principle which Colonel Haughton exemplified, it was – Stand by the rearguard to the last. He proved his fidelity to it at Saran Sar, at Tser Kandao, in the Dwatoi defile, and in the march down the Bara Valley; and he sealed it with his blood at Shinkamar. It was his motto, and for that man can do no more than die, if fate so wills.*"

Colonel Haughton's body was taken to Peshawar where it was buried with full military honours on 31 June 1898. A monument stands on the grave erected by 35th and 36th Sikhs at Peshawar.

This was also the end of the participation of 36th Sikh in the Tirah campaign. Including its gallant fight at Samana; they had two officers killed seven wounded, and 36 men killed 109 wounded.

The character of the remarkable CO of 36th Sikhs has been well amplified by Major A C Yate, "*I have written in the firm conviction that the memory and example of Colonel Haughton deserves to be remembered and kept in the army. To those who knew him best, he was a valued friend, to those whom he commanded, a trusted leader I now quote General Methuen who wrote in September 1899 "He struck me as one of the finest men I have ever seen, and his charm of manner never seemed to leave him. His coolness under fire and the manner in which he exposed himself was the admiration of every one, and I am quite certain, must have influenced the Afridis as well as ourselves. I can say no more, except that his end was full worthy of his life.*"

Undoubtedly, his commanding stature, coolness, capacity and resource must have left an imprint on the minds of the Afridis and Orakazais. He commanded a spirit and love of all that came into his contact. ***This then, was the leader who commanded exemplarily one of the best fighting soldiers, who established an iconic detail of valour, dedication, camaraderie, and achievements.***

SPOT WHERE LT COL J HAUGHTON DIED FIGHTING
SHIN KAMAR
29th January 1898

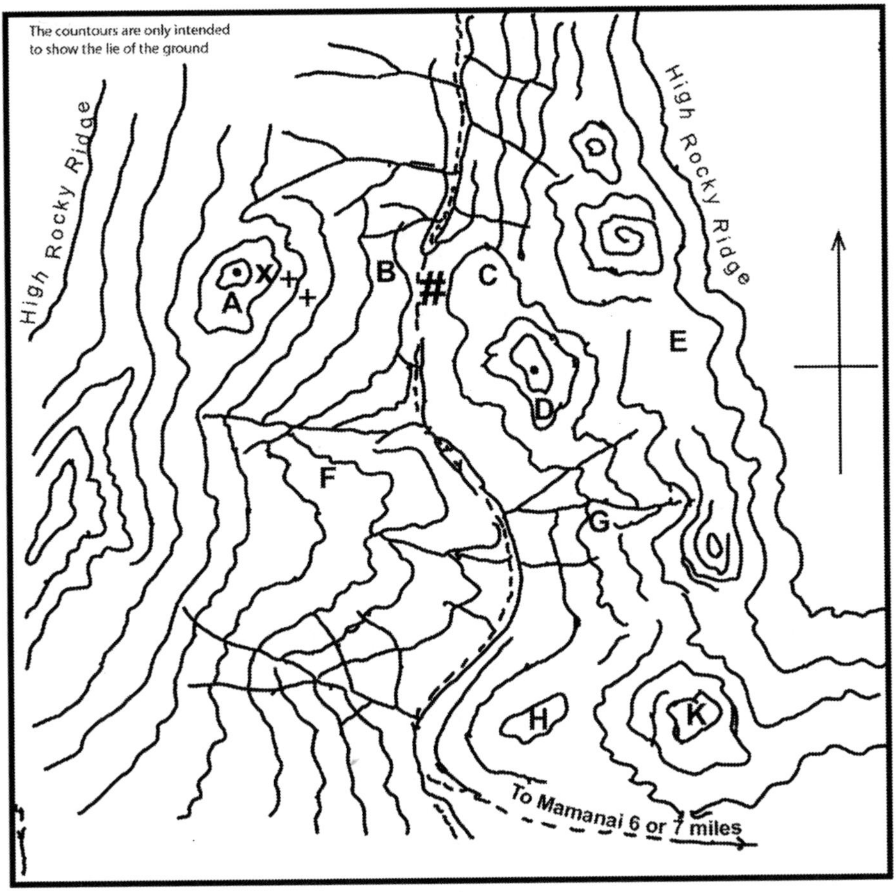

REFERENCES

A. 2 Companies York L.I B. 1 Company36th Sikhs C. 1 Company York L.I.

D.E.F.G.H.K Positions occupied by Companies York L.I during successive retirements.

X Spot where Lts. Dowdall and Walker fell.

++ Spot where Col. Haughton and Lt. Turning fell.

Crest of the Pass.

First Batch Of British Officers 36th Sikhs

Standing (R-L) Lt Craster, Lt Browne, 2/Lt Van Somere. Seated (R-L) Lt Munn, Capt Custance, Lt Col John Haughton, Maj Des Voeux, Capt Searle, Capt Surgeon Prall, IMS Lt. Turning

Lt Col J Haughton, CO 36th Sikh

Monument in Peshawar Cemetery

CHAPTER NINE

TACTICS

General

The genesis of the study of military actions lies in a thorough analysis of wars, campaigns and battles, seeing these with hindsight, to visualize the strategy and tactics employed and to draw out lessons for future warfare. The factors affecting tactics are primarily the terrain of the area involved, the character of adversaries, the weapons, equipment, logistics and other force multipliers used.

To also realize the Pathan perspective, their fighting techniques need to be studied. They understood the futility of fighting from fixed positions against the preponderance of British firepower. They adopted concentration for specific tasks to assault a fortified post. Otherwise, they mastered guerilla tactics. They made use of defiles, forested and close country for surprise rushes of knife wielding fighters that prevented the British from using fire support or command and control structures. The Pashtoons recognized the officers from their head dress and thus always endeavoured to pick them up.

About fighting in the Frontiers, Winston Churchill, who served as a Lieutenant during the Pathan revolt, said, *"Great and expansive forces, equipped with all the developments of scientific war, are harried and worried without rest or mercy by an impalpable cloud of active and well armed skirmishers. To enter the mountains and attack an Afridi is to jump into water to catch a fish."*

The Terrain

The Frontier is grim and romantic. Though the heights of features was mediocre, ranging up to 7000 feet, it was the tough terrain of loose stones, slippery boulders, sharp and steep ridges, precipitous cliffs, numerous ranges that were traversable from selected places only, recognized Kotal or Pass, and valleys full of gushing ice cold water that had to be negotiated again and again since the possible routes were only through them. There were hardly any roads and tracks to move on, and those in existence were of a very poor quality. New roads and tracks either had to be made or the existing ones improved upon. The distances involved from the resource and lines of communication were long, arduous and cumbersome. This required colossal effort and resources which were at a premium. There was hardly any local support available. All essential administrative echelons and logistics, had to be lugged forward in the tough going and subjected to disruptions by the tribesmen.

Hutchison summarized, *"Stern and wild: high mountains, precipitous cliffs, dangerous defiles, wild ravines and rushing torrents everywhere; while roads of any kind are conspicuous by their absence – a country, therefore, in which strict "formations" and precise "manoeuvres" as we find them described in our drill books, are impossible, and in which marches must be performed under conditions in which they become slow, exhausting professional movements, the long trailing flanks of which are dangerously exposed to attack from start to finish."*

Lightfooted Tribesmen

The Pathan was master of his grounds which he knew like the back of his palm. He moved light with rifle and knife and had incredible stamina. He was sharp witted, cunning, a natural fighter with a developed sense of opportunity. He was patient and thus waited for his chance to hit, while he utilized time to watch and reconnoiter. He did not fight a prolonged pitched battle anywhere, and used more of guerilla tactics and once engaged was reckless in his approach. He was content with small gains and quick returns. He fought an intense battle only at Dargai Heights that also losing ground too soon, and did not appreciate possibilities of fighting a stubborn resolute battle at tactically sound positions at crucial passes highly defencible viz; Sampagha, Arhanga and Saran Sar. He disliked having the enemy at high ground above him, having his line of retreat threatened, with artillery fire. His code was simple; a life for a life, an eye for an eye and a tooth for a tooth.

Adaptibility

Initially, the only match to the Pathan was a Gurkha since also from hilly terrain, he could climb steep slopes with ease, lay ambushes and beat the Pathans in their own game on the hills. They operated at night to counter Afghan snipers. Other races took time to acclimatize with the terrain and to watch the Pathan to understand him. Once done, were an equal match. Their discipline, regimentation, training and better management soon gave them equal prowess if not an edge over them. The Indians in the British Army were quick to adapt and carry their responsibilities with aplomb. Their management of collective fire power had a desired effect upon the Pathan. Their use of artillery, enmassed, or when required split to two guns at different places, paid high dividends. There were six mountain batteries that fired with precision having an excellent impact. These were massed for Dargai Heights, Sampagha and Arhanga.

Picketing

Picketing while on the move was soon mastered by the British. Most of the roads and tracks were through defiles or areas dominated by the hills. The ranges were elongated and hillocks numerous these had to be secured before the unwieldy columns moved forward. At times, these hillocks were held by the Pathans that required attack, capture and physical occupation. The advance guards and the rearguards had to learn by experience and hone their tactical approach.

Sniping

The tribesmen had adopted and refined their tactics of watching the British move into camps and safe positions at night. They would not fight a pitched battle. They would resort to sniping at sentries, patrols or camps after dusk and till early hours when they retreated to safer places. They kept the British on their toes day and night.

Use of Weapons

Apart from Jezails, the Pathans had acquired a very high number of Martin Henry rifles which they used with great skill. Some of these were stolen from the Amir's workshops, some imported from Birmingham or Belgium, and some stolen from the Levies. They also had Sniders Lee-Metfields and of course unlimited stock of ammunition. They had secured 50,000 rounds of ammunition from the Khyber forts. It was revealed that they had books on training in urdu. Some pensioners of levies and deserters had also joined their ranks providing great substance.

Harassing Tactics by the Tribesmen

They had developed a skill of hiding at lower heights and to bring on a fusillade of fire when the British went up the hills and their silhouette could easily be targeted. At Dwatoi and Bara Valley, the Afridis adopted the tactics of closing on the British soldiers, showering abuses and throwing stones to entice/induce them to show themselves, giving an opportunity to the snipers to engage them.

The tribesmen, when successful in skirmishes, became bolder and continued their actions with cunning and audaciousness. They developed the art of having patience, watching their prey, finding weakness and pouncing. They were generally routed but only after causing damage to the British.

Enveloping Tactics

The British employed enveloping tactics of attacking from two sides, thus exposing the enemy's flank. The successful examples are their operations against the Mohamands in Bajaur, and against Mahsuds when the British marched in four columns of enveloping movements.

Junior Leadership

Another essential was the juniors being able to fight on their own under trying circumstances, whether in an offensive or defensive battle. That meant need to build an inner character of steadfastness, resource and personal leadership. A glaring example was of posts at Samana, which fought gallantly under JCOs and senior NCOs. The paradigm set by Havildar Ishar Singh at Saragarhi is one of the most sterling examples where utmost trust was bestowed upon him, having been given the responsibility to command a band of soldiers under the most difficult circumstances, showed his initiative, resource and leading from the front at its best. Similarly, picketing, patrolling, guarding camps or baggage trails encompassed confidence on junior leaders. The wild landscapes presented opportunity to all to exercise their judgment quickly because it envisaged small unit actions whereby junior leaders were responsible for key decisions. There was demonstration of 'pluck and devotion' of the men, buoyancy, accurate appreciation and quick decisions of the officers, and the physical and mental robustness of all, which enabled them to face peculiar situations with resolute finish and elan, and emerge from them with success.

Role of Civil Officials

There was another facet that effected the planning, execution and fighting of the battles. Though it was the military pecking order that was responsible to carry out operations, there were civil officials having a great say as go-betweens. They had their own perceptions and influences which at times hampered military operations. They were found to be short of loyalty since they felt that after military operations it was they who had to deal with the populace. As such, many times they resorted to duplicity, prevailing upon the army to be less insensitive. Because of their negotiations, which entailed locals meeting them, the disagreeing tribesmen were always able to discern the military operations in the offing and the British invariably lost surprise, which was an important element of their tactics.

Flexibility in Employment of Artillery

The tribesmen were happy with smaller gains like having been able to inflict casualties upon the British forces. To deter them, the British also undertook operations to cause maximum casualties on the tribesmen who in British reckoning understood harsh language only. To achieve this, the British ensured maximum concentration of forces and artillery wherever feasible, to a greater degree, a policy to use a sledge hammer to crack a nut. This, however, was contradictory to the overall British policy of winning over the people for sustainable administration and areas as per their strategic and political aims.

Intelligence

Also, one of the most important essentials of success, the availability of information, was lacking. Topographical lack of information notwithstanding, any moves on formidable terrain imposed restrictions on tactics and logistics, thus nobody could predict actions or reactions of the tribesmen. The Political Officer, though might be having information, would be parochial at times, favouring the locals, a disadvantage to the British armed forces. The army had to protect itself whether in large or small numbers, thus slowing down their efforts for an aggressive and relentless approach.

The tribesmen though could concentrate large forces, but generally did not fight a pitched battle like an army. They had converted their houses into mini fortresses, from where the entire family fought, yet not of the nature of 'the last man the last round'. Whenever the British moved into their areas they had to face swarms of fighters, men, women and children. No direction could be left unprotected, necessitating all round protection. This hampered the need to press home forces at the point of decisive impact.

Protection during Move

During the move, there was an advance guard of two companies to a battalion. It was axiomatic during any move, advance or withdrawal, to assume that there might be an ambush laid at the next corner. They would move on hills on the sides, dispatching the piqueting troops at the highest dominating points. They had to ensure security of difficult points and approaches from where the tribesmen could make way to snipe at the moving columns. Most of the times, a battalion could do only a mile to three, another battalion taking over, thus leap-frogging, at a highly slow process. While doing so, wherever a larger enemy was found anywhere, the process required quick assemblage of forces, positioning of artillery and arranging for ammunition that took time. Meanwhile, the tribesmen would cause maximum damage and then move off, thus resorting to an inadvertent tactic of guerilla warfare. Move of a brigade group was the maximum that was possible. The harassment to the following troops enforced necessity of rearguards. Many a times, the advance guards also acted as rearguards, while their initial role was given to another body of troops. It had to be appreciated that there was no enemy army as such, but the enemy was the whole population.

Tactical Withdrawal

Once the operations were completed and the withdrawal was contemplated, the process of guarding had to be continued, with special emphasis on the rear as that fell to the fresh endeavours of the tribesmen.

It was so since the complete subjugation of the tribesmen could never be achieved by the British. The promises made by the *'Jirgas'* were violated by the Pathans with impunity, with or without commiseration of the *'Jirgas'*. The withdrawal, therefore, had to be coordinated even more methodically with great precision, lest the tribesmen took advantage to snipe at the vulnerable point at the most opportune time. This they did most masterfully.

Evacuation of Casualties

Another nightmare was clearing of casualties. A wounded soldier could not be left behind at the mercy of the tribesmen. There had been numerous cases in which the British troops captured were maltreated and bodies mutilated. This affected morale. The wounded could only be given a preliminary treatment at the spot, first aid or field bandage. Their evacuation demanded colossal effort, thus hampering the ongoing operations. *'Dhoolis'* were the prime mode of carriage of casualties. These were heavy and cumbersome, their brown tarpaulin showing as conspicuous targets. Ponies for the purpose were weak and untrained. The proportion of the wounded to the killed was 3:1, besides the ratio of the sick 11.16 percent of the Force.

The British had catered for 23 Field Hospitals, each capable of accommodating 100 sick men and were fully equipped, including supplies for three months. Hospitals were arranged at Rawalpindi, Nowshera and Kohat, with beds 3,000 beds or more.

Protection of Camps

At halts, the system was akin to one followed by the Americans in the West, when they moved from one place to another lock, stock and barrel. Their columns comprised of the complete families which included women, children and the old. The British adopted the parametric defence making small walls around and a low ditch inside along it. The fighting troops were placed along the perimeter and the administrative echelons in the center who were crowded, a good target for Afghan snipers. Congestion was of advantage to the tribesmen who never missed a target, once they fired from a reasonable range. It necessitated some troops to be deployed outside the perimeter at a fair distance from where the tribesmen could take potshots. Thus protection demanded two separate defence systems.

The tribesmen were not fond of pitched fighting at night. But they did resort to fire at night and at times running over the camps causing casualties.

Vigilance

All time alertness was a necessity to ward off sniping and raids by the tribesmen who had gained good expertise. In this, while the older units had gained experience, the new units tended to be either casual or lacked expertise and thus often suffered at the hands of the cunning foe who took full advantage of weaknesses.

As said earlier, the tribesmen did not like to operate at night, thus lost advantage of the possibility of using of the terrain they knew. On the contrary, the British took full advantage of their training and carried out movement, concentration and operations at night.

No unit could rest on its laurels, all-time vigilance was essential. Newly inducted units were watched by the tribals as soft targets.

The British strength was in its discipline, controlled fire and mutual support. Weakness was ignorance of the country and consequent tendency of small bodies to get detached.

Sum-up

Captain Nevill, summarized: *"The Afridis are essentially a fighting race...we have little to teach them in the tactics best suited to their conditions of organization and terrain. It is only in the higher branches of the art of war – the domain of strategy rather than tactics – that they have much to learn.... Lack of organization has always been the keynote of their guerilla tactics which have baffled again and again the armies of civilized nations."*

The prolonged hill warfare that the forces were subjected to taught them tactics and discipline experienced from physical combat with the brave and wily foe, the characteristic that became instinctive with the units who served in the frontiers. Harry Lumsden, the first commander of 'The Guides' who lived with the Pathans, laid down maxims *'to be alert and ready; to rise equal to the occasion, be the call small or great; to be not easily taken aback in a sudden emergency; to be a genial comrade.'*

CHAPTER TEN

THE LAST STAND

The history of the world is the study of wars fought in all regions of the world. The wars are decided by numerous battles that have impacted the outcome. There are numerous battles which have displayed spectacular feats of group or individual bravery and sacrifice. The heroism displayed demands enormous study and examination of the circumstances, the force levels, the leadership, and reasons for the men to fight so resolutely. There have been larger battles, skirmishes and campaigns in which the display of individuals and armies have seen awe inspiring feats of courage, fighting ability, resolute strength, agility, devotion and motivation, stamina and skills to use various weapons at hand. The effort here is not to explain larger battles, but restricted to examine some selected eminent and iconic actions, in light of the Battle of Saragarhi.

The field thus would be constricted to the literal meaning of 'the last stand' – a defensive action. Exemplary actions of other operations of war viz advance, attack or withdrawal, shall not form part of this analysis.

Then what is the 'last stand'? To eulogize feats of valour, various races, have sung paeans on the actions of their warriors or heroes. Parochialism has been the prominent bane. There have been numerous actions of bravery and sacrifice which would find a place in that category. Therefore, this study looks at mini actions – by smaller bodies resulting in acts of signal grandeur and military significance, and not the outstanding campaigns or large battles, fought by larger forces for prolonged periods.

The last stand in military parlance would be a circumstance where a small force in a defensive environment holds on to its responsibility (position) against an assault by larger and stronger force. The situations that can fall in this category can be holding out at some position of tactical significance, or defending a position entrusted to keep it intact, or refusal to give up a position of eminence. The defending band of men has to hold on to the position 'to the last man and the last round'. For this band of soldiers, withdrawing or surrendering is unthinkable, and finally its essence is to protect a cause.

The steadfastness of such a band of brave men, may have turned the tables on the attacker to undergo defeat or loss of valuable time.

In some situations, the defenders have surrendered or committed suicide rather than fight till the last. Thus have neither gained time nor inflicted losses on the enemy. This cannot form part of the 'last stand' as such. This aspect also should not be confused with surrender where knowing the enemy, there is hope of repatriation and thus 'better to live to fight another battle'. This situation gains credence when both belligerents have captured prisoners and thus there is hope of exchange, but obviously discarded for qualification to be 'the last stand'.

Notwithstanding a little digression to the literal meaning of "the last stand', some battles need mention because actions have been somewhat akin to the 'word', fought with meritorious ferociousness, bravery and total allegience to a cause.

The prevailing situation including topography, the type and strength of the enemy, the weapons, other force multipliers, the hopelessness of the situations in which the group fights may bring out the relative merit in tackling a particular situation that would allow examination of the action in its true perspective. However, to draw comparisons is not the aim here. The reader needs to visualize the actions in their totality and then draw their own conclusions and lessons.

Battle of Thermopylae. (08-10 September 480 BC). The battle was fought at Thermopylae – a pass in Greece. A force of 7,000 Greeks including 300 Spartans, blocked the Pass from the Persian army estimated to be numbering 1,50,000 to 2,00,000, ratio 1:285. The Greeks defended the position for several days before being overrun. These Greek soldiers have become a symbol of courage against overwhelming odds. Most of the defenders were killed establishing the power of patriotism in defending native soil. It is an inspirational example, in which the defenders facing certain death, particularly 300 Spartans who were placed on the Pass itself remained at the position till eliminated. They had been outflanked, due to treachery of a traitor, Ephiaites, who lead the Persians around the Pass, behind the Greek Army, thereby squashing any remote chance of Greek victory.

Siege of Numantia. In 300 BC, the Romans numbering 20,000 legionnaires, 40,000 allies and mercenary troops, surrounded the city of Numantia, held by Celtibarians. The siege lasted more than a year. The defenders withstood volumes of arrows unleashed by the Romans, till they died of wounds, starvation, and some suicides, but they refused to surrender.

Siege of Masada. In 74 CE, the troops of the Roman Empire lay siege to hilltop fortresses at Masada, in current day Israel, held by Jews, numbering 960. Unable to hold on, the Jews committed mass suicide, which became a symbol of Jewish resistance.

Battle of Alamo. This battle is a part of the Texan Revolution, fought in 1836 CE, from 23 February to 06 March. About 1800 Mexicans lay siege and then stormed a building held by 185-260 men of the Republic of Texas. 400-600 Mexicans were killed capturing the building against loss of 182-257 of the defenders, almost all of whom were killed. This battle is regarded akin to the battle of Thermopylae.

Custer's last Stand. On 25th June, 1876, this battle was a part of the Battle of Little Bighom. George Custor with a small force found himself on a hilltop when a large force of native Americans attacked them. The attackers suffered innumerable casualties but Custer's troops were destroyed within an hour.

Battle of Shiroyama. 24 September 1877 CE, about 500 Samurai of Satsuma were surrounded by 30,000 soldiers of the Imperial Japanese Army in Kagoshima, Japan. The Samurai held the position till their leaders were killed. Then they decided to charge the enemy downhill, all were killed inflicting far more casualties on the Japanese Imperial Army.

Battle of Rorke's Drift. On 22-23 January 1879 CE, 3-4000 Zulus were held by 141 British Army troops at Rorke's Drift at Buffalo River in South Africa on 28 October 1835. 350 Zulus were killed against 13 British. The Zulu attack was repulsed. Eleven Victoria Crosses were awarded, besides other decorations.

Battle of Concepcion. This battle was fought in 1882 CE. 77 Chilean soldiers were defending a garrison at Concepcion. They were attacked by 300 Peruvians, accompanied by 1000–1500 guerillas. The Chileans had entrenched themselves in a Church. They fought for 27 hours, eventually all the defenders were killed.

Battle of Shangani. On 25 October 1893 CE, during the First Metabela War, Zimbabwa, 34 soldiers of Shangani patrol were attacked by 5,000 Metabela warriors. The small band refused to surrender, at one stage fighting from behind the dead horses, till they ran out of ammunition. They killed 500 of the attackers. The Metabele soldiers were known to mutilate the bodies, but in this particular case they did not do so, saying 'the British fought so bravely we would not treat them as we do the cowardly Mashones and others.'

Battle of Tirad Pass. On 02 December 1899 CE, a rearguard of 60 Filipino soldiers fought a delaying action against 300 American soldiers, suffering 52 killed, and inflicting numerous casualties upon the enemy, allowing President Aguinaldo and his troops to escape.

Battle of Rezangla. During the Sino-Indian War of 1962, a Company of 13 Kumaon defended Rezangla Pass, Chushul Valley in Ladakh, at a height of 16,404 feet against assault by thousands of Chinese troops. 114 soldiers out of 123 Kumaonis were killed, nine were severely injured against the Chinese who suffered over 1,000 casualties. The Company Commander Major Shaitan Singh was awarded the Param Vir Chakra, posthumously. It is a grand example of collective bravery under an inspiring leader.

Battle of Walong. This battle was fought by troops of 4 Sikh at Walong, in 1962, against enveloping attacks of a far superior Chinese Force, both in number and resources. One of the platoons had all the men killed or wounded. The total casualties of 81 killed and 97 wounded and a few taken prisoners of war. Two out of four company commanders died and one was wounded.

Battle of Bumla. Bumla Pass, 37 km from Tawang in Arunachal Pradesh saw one of the fiercest battles during the Sino-India War of 1962. A platoon of 1 Sikh (now 4 Mech) fought most heroically under an outstanding leader Subedar Joginder Singh, who in spite of his grevious wounds killed many Chinese. He was taken prisoner of war and died in enemy custody and was awarded the Param Vir Chakra. The platoon beat back three enemy attacks and killed many Chinese before the superior enemy was able to capture the defences.

Battle of Longewala. During the Indo-Pak War of 1971, from 04 to 07 December, in the desert sector of the Western Front, One Company of 120 men of the Punjab regiment held a position at Longewala. The Company had one recoilless gun mounted on a jeep, while the Pakistanis had 45 Chinese T-59 tanks and US Shermans. The Company had laid some anti-tank mines in front of their defences. In the attack by thousands of Pakistanis, they lost 12 tanks and numerous soldiers. The next morning, the Indian Air force further destroyed 20 tanks and many Pak mechanized infantry vehicles. The resolute stand by the Indian soldiers is considered to be one of the most remarkable battles.

Battle of Saragarhi. Incredible story of 21 soldiers and a non-combatant of 36th Sikhs against thousands of Pathans, a staggering ratio of 1:476; unmatched and unprecedented. The post had been surrounded from all directions, yet knowing certain death, the men fought 'last round, last man', gaining a momentous tactical victory. All the 21 martyrs were awarded the Indian Order of Merit, then the highest award bestowed upon native troops, equal to the Victoria Cross, and India's Param Vir Chakra. But for the then policy of not awarding non-combatants, there would have, perhaps, been 22 awards.

> *"It is foolish and wrong to mourn the men who died. Rather we should thank God that such men lived."*
>
> – George S Patton

CHAPTER ELEVEN

WHY DO SOLDIERS FIGHT? WHY SIKHS (INDIANS) FOUGHT OTHERS' BATTLES?

In the Light of Martyrs of the Battle of Saragarhi

"The true soldier fights not because he hates what is in front of him, but because what is behind him."

– G K Chesterton

General

The heritage thinkers opine that '*Zar, Zameen and Zanani*' are basic causes of warfare; and that is true from epics of the Trojan War, the Ramayana and the Mahabharta.

We have already analysed the causes of war on the Frontier during 1870–1890s, and the effects and outcome. More or less, the same reasons prevail universally – political, social, territorial, economic, self-preservation or personal greed and attitudes. These human tendencies will perhaps continue. Keeping the overall analysis of wars and battles out of the preview of this postulation, my effort would be to concentrate on the human aspects of why men fight, give their best and sacrifice the ultimate. What are those fundamentals that actuate them to fight, expose themselves to wounds and death, set examples of chivalry, motivation and do deeds normally considered impossible.

This may thus fathom the understanding of the minds of the martyrs who fought at Saragarhi, knowing death was certain in an impossible situation they had been landed into.

Human Spirit

Man has a long history of intrigues, battles and wars. Numerous wars have had an impact on events and circumstances prevailing then and thereafter. The psychosis of fighting for some stimulating rationale for accomplishment of imaginative goals, due to certain developed attitudes is profound. People have fought iconic battles. What is that in the human spirit to sacrifice the ultimate? What is that urge, fire in the belly, amazing grit nourished through training, discipline, motivation and dedication that inspires him to embrace death against insurmountable odds? Detached and unbiased research would perhaps result in a study of the soldiers psyche through the mirror of those who were martyred at Saragarhi.

Stimulants

The question of why men fight has been analyzed by many thinkers, soldiers, psychologists and philosophers. The answers cover a multitude of diversifying perspectives. As it appears, there is no one reason to fight. Numerous factors come into play to rouse emotions that provoke a soldier to perform his best.

Instinct to Survive. The primitive years marked the instinct to fight to survive – satiate biological needs of hunger and sex. Herber Spencer had this to say, 'survival of the fittest'. Man learnt the art of hunting and defending himself from animals.

Exemplary Leaders. Another contributory aspect is that our culture dictates that because wars are inevitable, tough leaders are required to manage them: 'leaders favour war because war favours leaders'. *Most officers embrace the military system out of romantic attraction to authoritarianism, a totalitarian lifestyle and military machismo. They are stripped of freedom as it is drilled into them they are superior, when they obey orders without question. Regimentation, political indoctrination and military administration are drilled into them.*

Evoking Emotions. The military leaders lead their men into battle with a commitment, with a right bestowed upon them by an authority, emanating from the head of the governing body down the chain of command. They fight to obey orders – equate morality with absolute obedience. The state has its own logic to commit forces at its command to wage wars and fight battles. Further logic and rationale to fight is provided by the leaders – civil or military. Logic does not motivate men as such when in the face of death. This is where the leader uses his leadership qualities to shroud logic and evoke emotions. Where reason fails, emotions prevail. Leaders thus have to rouse the emotions of their men to do the ultimate.

Evoking a sense of Righteousness. Human nature is defensive. To defend, aggressiveness ensues. Logic weakens its aggressiveness and thus contributes to meekness. It is at this juncture that a leader fogs logic and instead evokes emotions. While the leader continues to plan and execute by logic and rationale, not blinded by emotions, the men are afflicted by the arousal. The men, therefore, execute what a normal human does not endeavour to do. Soldiers fight for their duty and responsibility. They are entrusted to fight all challenges because the authority to protect their system has been challenged. Authority to defend and protect has been entrusted to them which they cherish and are prepared to kill or be killed. Similarly, they attack because they are entrusted to do so to capture areas important for the authorities. They kill because that has to be done to capture and annihilate the foe working against their authority that laid the ground rules for them.

The stirring element thus according to Tennyson, *'Theirs not to make reply, Theirs not to reason why, Theirs but to do and die'*.

The necessary transgression to appreciate the overall picture now takes us back to the nitty gritty that constitute a state of mind to fight and give out the best.

Pariotism and Obligation. The fight for satisfaction of hunger and sex, furthered to defend the mate, hence graduation to cave, den and herm that the civilization took its roots. There emerged an element of ownership and obligation to defend it, hence patriotism. Tribes, hutments, villages, cities and territorial principalities were set up. There evolved fighting as groups, under chieftains and patriarchs, – strong, wealthy and virile. They were groomed or born to be leaders as best warriors or from ruling ancestry.

Escape from Monotony to do the Honourable. There were those young men who were not happy with the patriarchic system and did not accept the family hierarchy, and did not like to till the land or were not happy to study, hence to escape from all this they preferred recruitment in the armed forces. They felt bored, and suffocated at home. They joined the military to fulfil their dreams which they lacked in their community. There was an element of rebellion in their traits, and to satisfy the same, they accepted a tough life and lure of combat. They fought to defend or to achieve more. They returned from near and far lands with riches, uniforms, spectacular accruements and medals to flaunt, and romantic stories of new lands and of valour that induced the young to follow. There was also the added advantage of pay and honourable acceptance in society. They thrilled in the adulation given to them.

Rejection of Fear. Another aspect of acts of bravery beyond the call of duty, is also the reaction to an extremely difficult situation, when cornered, resulting in fear creeping in. Fear makes a person either flee or surrender, or fight to survive and kill. This characteristic is more prominent and relevant in individuals than a band of people, particularly when in grained in the spirit of organized fighting.

> *"In war, the chief incalculable is the human will."*
>
> – B H Liddle Hart

Group Cohesion. There is universality in warfare that 'group consistency' and 'esprit de corps' are inculcated among soldiers through living and training together in sub-groups, units and regiments. This is a goading feature for men to fight together and accomplish jointly. Popular literature and veterans' stories are filled with anecdotes of men fighting because they loved and cared for the men in their units. Added to this were the 'paeans' sung for valour and sacrifice.

Tales and Examples of Predecessors. The emotional brass tacks that cause impulses in men to suffer wounds and death therefore are appetite, sex, self-preservation, greed for more, ambition, monotony, seeking recognition, romance for duel and religious fervor ignited or inspired by their predecessors or contemporaries who have won laurels. The romance of selfless heroism germinates and magnifies on the spur of the moment. The vision that if they win and return safe, they would be respected; if wounded they shall be taken care of and if killed shall be recognized and their families looked after.

Training, Regimentation and Glory. Training builds up automatic reflexes to deal with perceived or 'thrust upon' situations. They perform subconsciously, assimilating flexibility in approach. The rigours of training, the hammering in of aspects of honour, patriotism, fighting for colleagues, the sub unit, unit, regiment and country bring out the best in them. It is pride and glory that manifest to impell soldiers to give out their best at the time of calling.

Bonds of Kinship, kindling Honour. The men from the same village, towns, areas and country as such would fight for prestige, lest they lose face at places they or their families are known. The inflaming of their minds for honour to race and religion are maximum derivatives for emotional arousal. The examples drilled in the mind of natural leaders and fighters whose iconic acts, and the recognition and the awards conferred for their deeds, arouse a spirit to emulate. Soldiers fight to stay alive. They fight to keep their fellow soldiers alive. Rage further induces fury. A view is expressed by Lt Col Harold G Moore as: *'Troops in battle don't fight for what some President says. They don't fight for mom, the flag or apple pie. They fight for one another. And they become brothers for life.'*

Morality Imbibed. The education and assertions made by own people – political, social, economic and religious systems to be the best – and that the foe is bad, virtueless, balatantly guilty of atrocities on the innocent, ungodly and ungallant – act to build a spirit to fight to take revenge, teach a lesson to the perpetrators and annihilate them. Alluring and refined justifications and dogmas are coined and are impressed upon their yet immature minds to bring in attitudinal traits to follow a specified line. The discontentment of physiological and psychological needs provide the fuel.

> *"Of all the passions that inspire a man in a battle, none, we have to admit, is so powerful and so constant as the longing for honour and reknown."*
>
> – Carl von Clauswitz

Inspirational Factors of Saragarhi Heroes

The motivators for war are as varied as the type of people that fight them. This takes us to an analysis of factors that perhaps inspired the men to fight to the end at the Saragarhi Post.

(a) All the men hailed from the same areas of recruitment in erstwhile Punjab, the Malwa region. Their predecessors had fought wars.

The stories of the acts of bravery and sacrifice were already rife. All of them were from the peasantry, hardy and enduring.

(b) All the men were from the same sub-unit, unit and regiment. Those who came from other units had brought richness of knowledge and expertise. Those who were recruited on re-raising of the unit were young, enthusiastic and full of dreams.

(c) They belonged to the same religion – Sikhism. All had heard stories of sacrifices of their Gurus. They adored and were ingrained with the tenets of the Sikh faith.

(d) The ballads, paeans, stories of valour of Gurus, Bachhitar Singh, Banda Bahadur, Baghel Singh, unparalleled Maharaja Ranjit Singh, Hari Singh Nalwa, Akali Phoola Singh, Zorawar Singh, Mohkam Chand and many others inspired them to no end.

(e) They had spent almost two years in the same area before being asked to defend Saragarhi, hence knew the terrain and the foe. They had certainly developed a sense of superiority.

(f) They had belief in British leader, who led from the front, knew and respected their language, areas, religion and customs.

(g) They realized the power of no-nonsense leadership of their immediate boss – experienced, formidable, awe inspiring, empathetic, humane and brave leader of Spartan attitude – the father figure of Havildar Ishar Singh.

(h) They believed in the cause of keeping the Frontiers in check as was done by Hari Singh Nalwa under Maharaja Ranjit Singh to keep their own territories safe.

(j) They realized the requirement of defending the Saragarhi Post at all costs, since its importance lay in keeping up communications between the two main forts of Gulistan and Lockhart, also the tactical necessity of keeping the gap in the Samana defence system well covered.

(k) They were living, feeding, playing and fighting together hence natural buddies through hell and fire.

Why Sikhs (Indians) Fought Others Battles

A question is often raised as to why the band of soldiers at Saragarhi fought so dedicatedly. Why didn't they succumb to the lure and latitude provided by the Afghan General Gul Badshah? He had told them in absolute terms that they were fighting someone elses battle, that of the British. They were told that if they abandoned fighting they will be allowed to go to Kohat and their homes safely. Was this offer given right at the beginning of the fight or during the battle when they were not achieving much and were suffering casualties is a matter not very clear. But the offer was made a fact, duly substantiated by the locals.

But then, it was not the Sikhs at Saragarhi only who were fighting so bravely, it was all along the Samana Ridge. Numerous other units who fought battles bravely for the British in the Frontiers also had Sikhs in varying percentages. It was so with all the brave Indian races that fought gallantly; even thousands of tribesmen, recruited by the British to defend their interests on the Frontier.

The Indians, who fought for the British voluntarily, did so with the rationale of the profession of a soldier, motivating factors for which have already been discussed. Circumstances at home, psychology, military lures, hero-worship, regimentation, favourable policies of the British and good leadership were the reasons that provided fodder for the Indians to fight for the British.

Another angle, however, requires analysis. For years, the Muslims had invaded India, through Punjab. The main brunt of their onslaught was always felt most severely by the people of Punjab. For decades they had sacrificed for their lands, values, hearth, and homes. The British provided them an opportunity to fight back the marauders who had plundered their country and had perpetrated uncountable atrocities.

It was the trained, disciplined and motivated forces of numerous Indian races under the highly able generals of Maharaja Ranjit Singh, who had for the first time turned tables and advanced West subjugating territories belonging to the invaders. As the time passed, the psyche of the Indians advancing into Frontiers or Afghanistan started believing those were their lands. The argument took force in young minds who believed steadfastly that all that Maharaja Ranjit Singh held or where the Sikh Empire had its sway belonged to them. Those who fought at Saragarhi were grained with the belief that they were defending their own lands. Faith spurred their motivation to fight to 'the last man last round' with grit, determination, cool composure and meticulous battle, not only to sacrifice but to annihilate maximum of the enemy.

To quote words of Lt Col John Haughton suggest a well thought out strategy to play upon the dislike by the Sikhs of the Afghans, viz: "*A suggestion has been made that the Sikhs, the hereditary foes of the Pathans, should be planted along the borders in posts, or small colonies, and that to them a free hand should be given to check Pathan raids. The suggestion appears to have attracted no official attention, but that does not argue its impossibility or worthlessness.*"

> "*If you don't fight for what you want,*
> *Don't cry for what you lost*"
>
> – Bhagwat Geeta

CHAPTER TWELVE

SOME DETERMINANTS

Durand Line: Jurisprudence

Countries and people have been divided through lines and borders drawn with questionable justification. If justifications and viability suited a situation at the time of division or demarcation, and resulted amity, satisfaction and progress, then it is worth its while. Yet, in most cases, where lines have been drawn out of personal, individualistic and irrational arguments serving the aggressive, assertive and hegimonious nations with results of resentment, repercussions and volatility, then and thereafter, the divisions stand liable to scrutiny. The bleeding from such cuts imposed have had rupturing, rambling and reoccurring eruptive sores that became cancerous.

The Durand Line was one such geopolitical and geostrategic recklessness or wisdom-gone-awry that manifested into unmatched and unwanted distress and misery.

The irony was that both sides were in unison, the Amir Abdur Rehman initiated need of a clear defined border while the British dreamt of a buffer state against Russian expansion towards Central Asia. The Amir insisted upon independence in his internal affairs, yet was prepared, reluctantly though, to forego control on foreign affairs. A clear line thus suited both. While the two tried for solutions, the dagger drawn by them sliced through a body whose self-rights were ignored and butchered.

The Russian threat had petered out to a greater extent – a result of demarcation affected by the Russo-Anglo Joint Boundary Commission in November 1893, by drawing a clear cut border between Russia and

Afghanistan. Yet, there was palpability of the Amir desiring a dividing line with the British who in turn had own self evoking-designs of ensuring a strong and opaque buffer.

To this effect, the Amir wrote to Lord Dufferin, the Viceroy of India. Finding a lukewarm response the Amir, wrote to the Secretary of the State of India, Viscount Cross. The mistrust and miscommunication in the parleys, however, was resolved by the new Viceroy, Lord Lansdowne. Lord (General) Roberts, who had fought in the Second Anglo-Afghan War, lead a commission to Kabul. The Amir suspected difficulty to negotiate with him, hence dilly dallied in accepting the mission, which prompted the British to send out an ultimatum, browbeating the Amir to seek pacification. The Amir asked for a map giving proposal of the boundary, in a letter that he was known to have intentionally delayed in reaching the British till General Roberts reverted to England.

The mistrust continued since the Amir found the mischief of exclusion of some territories that he felt to be part of his state. These were Waziristan, New Chaman, Chageh, Bulund Khel. Mohmand, Asmared Chitral. He wrote a conciliatory letter:

> *"...if you...Cut them out of my dominions, they will neither be of any use to you or to me: you will always be engaged in fighting or other troubles with them, and they will always go on plundering. As long as your Government is strong and in peace, you will be able to keep them by a strong hand, but if any time a foreign enemy appears on the borders of India, these frontier tribes will be your worst enemies.... In your cutting away from me these frontier tribes, who are people of my nationality and my religion, you will injure my prestige in the eyes of my subjects, and will make me weak, and my weakness is injurious to your Government."*

Was this the anguish of a genuine, helpless beleaguered ruler or mischief of a bigot playing truant?

As a response, the British occupied some areas viz, Bulund Khel and Wana Zhob. Tensions notwithstanding, the British sent a mission under Sir Henry Mortimer Durand, reaching Kabul on 02 October 1893 that was well received. The negotiations were amicable. The Durand Line Agreement was signed on 13 November 1893.

It is said that the Amir organized a public gathering at which he praised the Agreement and he accepted it with pleasure and satisfaction. He even thanked Sir Henry Durand. Yet there is another version held by known historians H L Nevill and James W Spain, that there was resentment and contradictions by the Amir since he apprehended that the British will nibble their part of so called 'sphere of influence' thus nibbling the 'virtual buffer' with an eye on the other half. The tribesmen felt cheated as both sides had connived to end their 'jealously guarded independence'. Where as their affinity to the Amir gave them some comfort, but the British manoeuvers was intolerable.

The Joint Commissions of both the sides were set in with the task of physical demarcation. The Amirs reluctance was apparent when the acceptance of providing security to the demarcation parties was not done to the extent expected. The Amir also, perhaps, indulged in rousing the feelings of the tribesmen to a pitch that resulted in an uprising in 1897.

Thus, while demarcation was successfully implemented elsewhere pillars were erected or an understanding along the prominent geographical features was reached the Mohmand territory including Bohai Bag was annexed by the British.

Demarcation or division of what? An area inhabited by the indigenous Pashtuns, recognized as such since 500 B.C., as mentioned by the Greek historian Herodotus about people called 'Pactyans' living around Arachosia, an area West of the Indus River. The Arabs conquered, introduced Islam as back as the 7th Century, and became a part and parcel of the lands they adopted. The route through this area towards India was taken by the Persian conqueror Darius in 516 B.C. Alexander of Macedonia came in 326 B.C. followed by Muslim armies under Qutaybs ibn Muslim in 705, Mahmoud Ghazni in 1001, Muhammad Gauri in 1175 and Ghengis Khan in 1213. Timur came in 1383 and his descendent Babur in 1526. Ahmad Shah Durrani attempted to conquer Punjab in 1748. The Sikhs '*Misaldars*' (clan chiefs) turned tables and invaded from the Southeast in 1813. The British followed in retaining what the Sikhs had captured, and tried to expand further.

The First Anglo-Afghan War of 1839, defeat of the British in 1842, the Second Anglo-Afghan War in 1878 with attainment of some geographical objectives by the British and finally demarcation of the Durand Line and its details have already been recorded in earlier chapter.

The original document was written in English, with translated copies in *'Dari'* and *'Pashto'*. The so called NWFP included areas of Multan, Mianwali, Bahawalpur and Dera Ghazi Khan. These were one time part of the Durrani Empire from 1709 to 1820, when the Sikh Empire was spread to include these areas, later secured by the British, with additional areas captured.

Thus, as we see that Afghanistan had become a pawn in the 'Great Game' between the Russians and Great Britain for control of Central Asia. Great Britain invaded Afghanistan to counter Russia. In fact, both had moved into Afghanistan or the Frontier for their self-interests. They precluded legitimacy of the righteous. The issue was stretched to the Durand Line ensuring a thin strip of Afghanistan running to the Chinese border, thus separating the two chief protagonists.

Therefore, the self interest of the adversaries subjugated a people thriving in their independence. The British hegemony and efforts to put forward arguments of its righteousness by advocating the idea to protect its territories from Russian expansion and to improve the lot of the tribesmen through progressive measures was a farce. It was to mask the psychic anarchy let loose for years that started when East India tasted blood in pursuing a policy of securing territories and then the British Government itself getting into the game. The idea bleeds several nations even today; the areas involved being the hottest flash points.

The British psyche of hegemony, pulsating audacity and façade of self righteousness is best illustrated by quoting words of Lord Macaulay's address to the British Parliament on 02 February 1835: *"I have travelled across the length and breadth of India and I have not seen one person who is a beggar, who is a thief or such wealth I have seen in this country, such high moral values, people of such caliber, that I do not think we would ever conquer this country, unless we break the very backbone of this nation, which is her spiritual and cultural heritage and therefore, I propose we replace her old and ancient culture system, her culture, for if the Indians think that all that is foreign and English is good and greater than their own, they will lose their self esteem, their native culture and they will become what we want them, a truly dominated nation."*

PERSONAL EQUIPMENT OF THE BRITISH AND INDIAN SOLDIERS

Dress. In 1870-90s, the British wore a scarlet jacket, blue trousers which had a red stripe on the sides along the legs, and a white helmet. Some units in India however, wore khaki uniform from 1885, which in 1896 was instituted for all units in combat. British troops wore pitch helmets while Indians mostly wore turbans. Gurkhas wore pill box hats. Scotch Highlanders wore the kilts and the light infantry tartan trews.

Organisation of an Infantry Battalion. A British Infantry Battalion comprised 10 companies with around 700 men and some 300 offcers in all ranks. A battalion had a maxim machine gun detachment of two guns and 20 men. Indian infantry battalions had the same composition except maxims. Senior officers were Britishers holding Queen's Commissions, a battalion having five or six; junior officers were Indians. The three Presidencies were incorporated into a single force in 1895.

Equipment. An infantry soldier carried a load of 33 lbs, without weapon and ammunition, which included a spare shirt and trousers, drawers, socks, greatcoat and personal toiletries bundled into a blanket and a cape waterproof, weighing 14 lbs. Besides, he had a mess-tin, a two pint canteen, boots and clothing weighing 12 lbs. Added was an entrenching tool used as pick and shovel weighing 3 lbs. He, in field, carried cooked rations, generally biscuits, weighing 2 lbs. (The author on his commission in 1962 used the same weapons and equipment).

Arms and Ammunition. There were different kinds of rifles in service; however, the Indian soldier carried a Martini-Henry rifle with 40 to 50 rounds of ammunition in a bandolier (pouch). In some cases, a soldier carried two bandoliers, 40 and 10 rounds. Officers carried swords, revolvers and telescopes in place of rifles. Second line of ammunition, 40-50 rounds, was also introduced which however was not a part of the ammunition that was carried on person.

Swords and Spears. Other arms and services except infantry, also carried an assortment of swords, light and bent, heavy and straight, and long or short lances – with bamboo or ash shaft carried by cavalry.

Rifle. The men of 36th Sikhs carried a Martini rifle. It was England's first field rifle. About the rifle, Rudyard Kipling had to say in his book 'The Young British Soldier':

> *"When 'arf of your bullets fly wide in the dirch,*
> *Don't call your Martini a cross-eyed bitch.*
> *She's human as you are – you treat her as sich,*
> *An' shall fight for the young British soldiers."*

The rifle was designed as breech-loading, self-cocking, rear-locking, lever-operated single-shot bolt action. The weapon was stout. It was designed by Friedrick von Martini of Switzerland. The barrel had a rifling system, having seven grooves, designed by Alexander Henry. It had an external hammer to strike the firing pin for ignition. Later, with the development of Metford system, these weapons were also referred to as Martini-Enfields or Martini-Metford. The rifle had variations Mark I, II, III and IV. Crown, manufacturing markings, year and Mark were stamped on the right side of the stock as identification marks. A safety on the cocking piece and a half-cocking bolt position were designed to provide security against accidental fire. On the left side of the fore-stock, there was a long range sight in the form of a dial that could be rotated to align with a circular hole in an upward raised aperture sight.

The rifle had a short chamber Boxer-Henry .45 caliber black powder cartridge. The thin sheet of brass rolled around a mandrel was soldered to an iron base. These cartridges were weak and got damaged and hence were later replaced by solid brass. The carbines of the time were also on the same pattern but bullets were lighter. Martini-Henry Mark IV were of .402 caliber. A cleaning rod was carried below the barrel, inserted into the butt-stock. The rifle had a 12 inches long bayonet in front. A magazine could be filled with eight or ten rounds.

The British troops were armed with a relatively new Lee-Metford, later Lee-Enfield rifle of .303 calibre. It had a magazine and smokeless propellent.

Artillery. Both British and Indian Royal Artillery Batteries had Rifled Muzzle Loading (RML) 2.5 inch gun (nick named 'screw gun', as the barrel was in two sections for easy carry in transport or mules, and would be screwed up for firing).

BATTLE CRIES

To get into frenzy, to fight to his best, a soldier shouts or yells his unit's 'battle cry'. It has been categorized as manly trait. It is a sense of aggression which increases a person's adrenal to physical violence.

Psychologically, a roar, snort, screeching, grunt or shouting are the acts of showing prowess to the adversary to make him cow down and back out. It can be termed as avoiding a conflict to soar in physical squabble, thus avoiding self injury. But if it does not work out favourably, the person fights bodily, drawing inspiration from the guttural or loud voices he produces. This basic human nature, when organized into a team slogan, essentially evokes a will-to-fight syndrome. In it there is an element of exploitation intended to get the best of soldiers in a military situation or action.

A rehearsed joint howl or a piercing shout aimed to intimidate the adversary to chill out is termed as 'war cry'. To the enemy, it is a nerve-wrecking message that may sound like a drowning roar and frenzy of a maddened elephant. Bands of warriors or soldiers crying out in unison aggressively are to frighten the enemy. Thus animal streak of human beings is tapped to boost own motivation, escalating the output.

Each race, region, country has its own slogan to embellish sense of pride of its tradition, culture, values, possessions or family. There are those who want to increase their influence. It is not possible to weigh a plethora of such war cries, however an effort is being made to discuss some having blood-curdling effect, in the light of the battle of Saragarhi. The selection endeavours to bring out variation. No effort shall be made to compare, only the description and the rest is left to the imagination of the reader.

Slogans (War Cries) by Foreign Armies

'Barritus'. The Romans used this martial growl, hard tone and a hoarse murmur, by putting their shields before their mouths to make the voice full and deep. Whereas it kindled courage in Romans, it struck fear in the foe.

'Oorah'. It perhaps is a descent from 'Hurrah", which was put into great effect by the Americans and the British.

'Rebel Yell'. It was developed by the Confederate soldiers during the American Civil War, to boost own morale and terrorize the enemy.

'Uukhai' or 'Hurray'. This slogan was used by the Mongols, holding hands out with palms up and move them thrice in clock-wise circle.

'Deus Vult'. During the 'First Crusade', the Christians used this war cry against the Muslims for their 'Holy Land'. The slogan meant 'God wills it'.

'Urrah'. This has been the slogan of the Russians.

'Alala'. This was the slogan of ancient Greeks, seeking blessings of 'Alala', the 'Goddess of War'.

'Banzai'. The Japanese soldiers shout 'Tenno Heika Banzai', 'Long Live the King'.

'Ei! Ei! Oh!' The Japanese samurai used this growl.

'Hakka Paalle'. The Light Cavalrymen of Finland shouted the slogan, meaning, 'Cut them down'.

'The Sword of the Lord, and of Gideon'. Gideon had led 300 men to the Midianite Camp carrying horns and torches, shouting the slogan.

'Allahu Akbar'. This war cry is by the Muslims, meaning 'God is Great'.

War Cries by Indian Soldiers

Today India has many regiments from different regions of a vast country. Different races have adopted slogans or war cries according to their own customs and beliefs. Each slogan has a solemn meaning and is as piercing as the other. However, here only those slogans would be referred to as pertaining to the time, especially during the period 1870s to 1890s.

'Veera madras, adi kollu, adi kollu'. It is by the soldiers from Madras, meaning 'Brave Madrasi, hit and kill, hit and kill'.

'Badri Vishal Lall ki Jai'. This is the slogan of the soldiers from Garhwal, meaning 'Victory to the Great Lord Badri Nath'.

'Jaya Mahakali, Ayo Gurkhali'. It is by the Gurkhas of Nepal as well as India, meaning, 'Glory to Great Kali, the Gurkhas Approach'.

'Jai Bajrang Bali'. By the soldiers of Bihar meaning, 'Victory to Lord Hanuman'.

'Bol Jawala Ma ki Jai'. By the Dogras, meaning, 'Say Victory to Goddess Jawala'.

'Jat Balwan, Jai Bhagwan'. It is slogan of the Jat regiment meaning 'Jat brave, victory to God."

'Raja Ram Chander ki Jai'. By Rajputana Rifles 'Victory unto Raja Ram Chander'.

'Chatrapati Shivaji Maharaj ki Jai'. It is the war cry of the Mahrattas, 'Victory onto Chatrapati Shivaji Maharaj'.

'Veer Bhogya Vasundra'. 'The brave shall rule the earth' is by manyartillery units.

'Bole so Nihal, Sat Sri Akal'. By the Sikhs, a slogan vision of Guru Gobind Singh, meaning 'He who cries God is Truth is ever Happy'.

DRESS AND WEAPONS OF THE AFGHANS

Dress

The men wore a traditional 'Pashtoon' dress, a loose fitting shirt of some coarse cloth, called *'Qmis'*, which reached the knees and a *'Salwar'*, full trousers tied at the waist with a string. A vest was worn over the shirt. Footwear was a *'Chaplay'*, sort of thick leather flip-flops, with a strong strip behind the heel to secure it. Males wore a *'Pagri'* (turban). Long strips of cotton cloth were wound round the head, sometimes over a *'Topi'* (cap). One end of the turban, about eight inches long, often was left standing upright over the turban and a yard long end dangling over the shoulder. The latter was often used to wipe the face. They also wore a *'Chadar'* (long piece of wide cloth), especially in winters, wrapped around their shoulders. Some men (especially) the young, also wore a woolen cap called *'Pakol'*.

The turban described a person's title, age, status, closely associated with the culture and religion.

The women wore baggy black or coloured trousers, a long shirt belted with a sash, and a long cloth over the head. Over it, they usually wore a *'Burqa'* – a veil that covered them head to knees.

Weapons

The Afghans carried rifles, swords or spears. The Jezail, a musket (rifle) was the main stay.

The Jezail was the main weapon used by the tribesmen with a great effect. It was flint lock type with a crude butt stock. It was a long barreled weapon almost six feet long without the bayonets, which rested on two places. It could be fired effectively from a distance of 800 yards with fair accuracy. The weapon was mainly made by the Adam Khel Afridis of Kohat craftsmen. The Jezail was superior to the Brunswick rifle that was used by some Indian troops, but less effective than the Martinis.

The Pathans also had service rifles which had been stolen from units stationed on the Frontier. They had also collected rifles from Afghanistan that had been discarded by the Continental armies besides those stolen from the Amir's armouries. The locals in British service, who deserted with their weapons, joined the Pathan ranks. Those rifles requiring repairs or refitting, were done up by the Afridi craftsmen who were masters of the art.

The stocks, barrels and other components were hand-made and beautifully decorated with carvings and paint work. The Afghans used these weapons very effectively from cliffs and defiles. The impact was devastating on the British Armies.

Since the Jazails had long barrels, they were used from horseback, as butt kept on the ground the muzzle reached the shoulder of the rider and thus easy to reload. The musket had a horn or bipod to steady the barrel while the butt was so shaped to fire from the shoulder and while riding a horse or a camel was pressed hard under the arm.

BRITISH AND AFGHAN WEAPONS

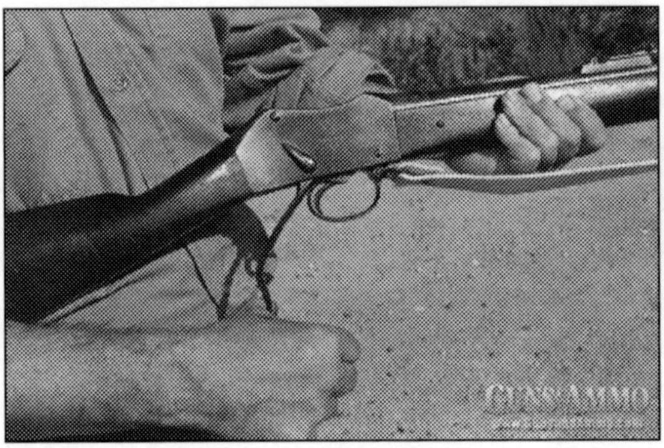

Rifle Martini Henry

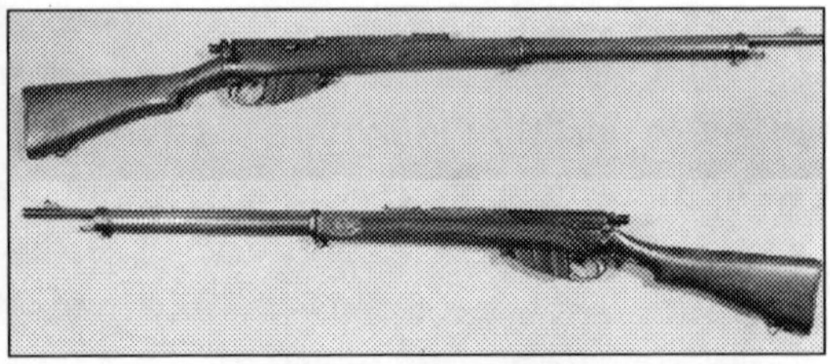

Rifle Lee Metford

RML 2.5 inch Mountain Gun 1895

RML 7 pounder
Mountain Gun 1895

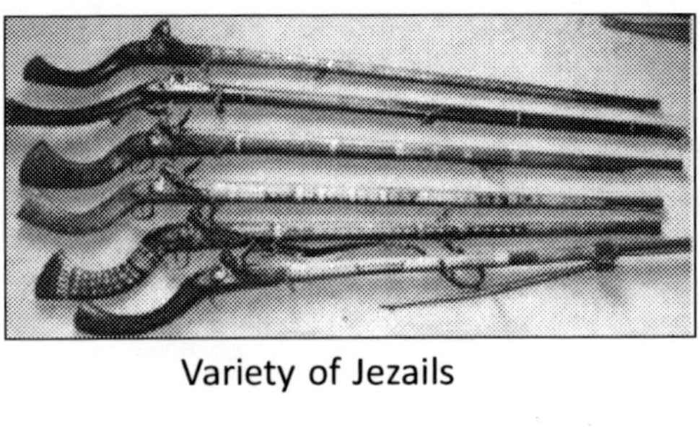

Variety of Jezails

Jezail Mounted on Bipod

DETERMINANTS

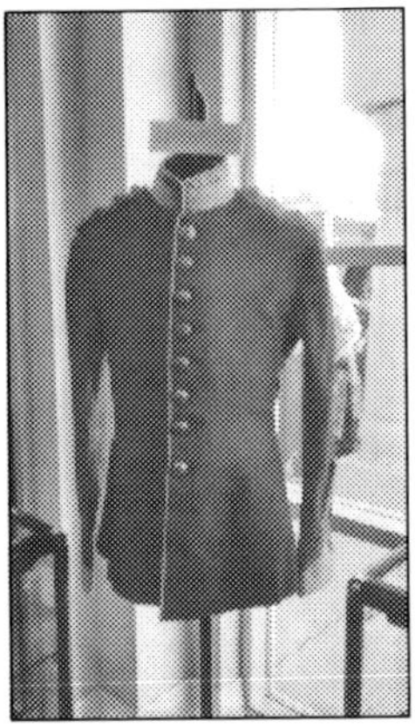

Ceremonial Uniform Jacket

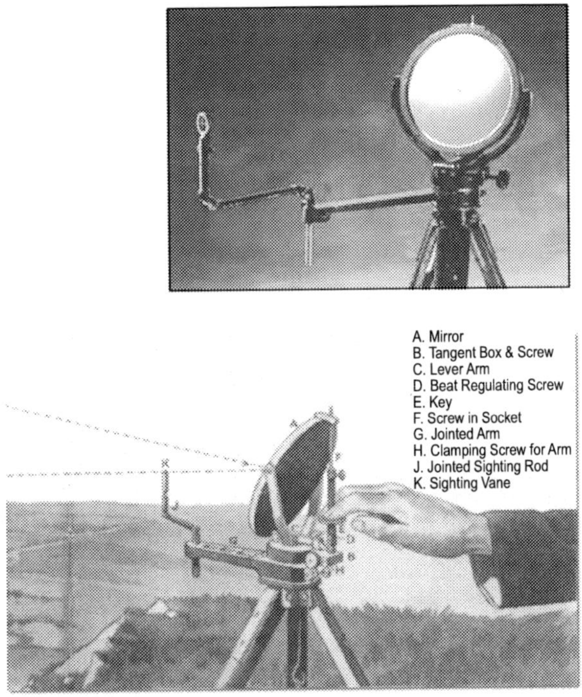

Heliograph

IOM

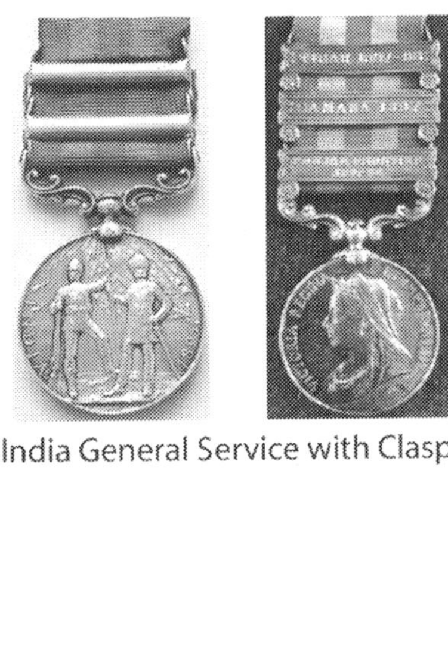

India General Service with Clasps

CHAPTER THIRTEEN

36 SIKHS: 4 SIKH AFTER 1898

General

It would be appropriate to complete the sequel of the epic of Saragarhi by narrating of history 4 Sikh after 1898. 36 Sikhs was fortunate to have participated in almost all the major wars, battles and insurgencies. In each it has excelled in every way-bringing laurels that need to be highlighted. While up to 1947, the Unit fought 'others' battles' thereafter it fought magnificently under its own 'Tricolour', the highly venerated independent Bharat's ***'Nishan'***.

The chronicle for the above would need a book by itself, a sequel to 'Saragarhi Battalion – Ashes to Glory' by the author of this book. But for the present, a very brief history of the entire 121 years would suffice to analyze the psyche and ethos of 36th Sikhs, which is totally imbued with understanding of the cause, raw courage and steadfastness in battle.

The story is narrated period-wise.

1898 to 1913

Normal barrack routine was interspersed with exercises, visits and inspections. In 1900, the Regiment carried out escort duties at Chitral, and then moved to form part of the Malakand Force. On 21 Nov 1905, it participated in the review by HRH, the Prince of Wales at Rawalpindi. In 1905, it was rearmed with the Magazine Lee Enfield Rifle, later to be replaced by the new short Lee Enfield Rifles.

Three Memorials were erected at Amritsar, Samana and Ferozepur in November 1901, April 1902 and January 1904, respectively. The title of the

Regiment was changed from '36th Sikh Infantry' to 36th Sikh on 02 October 1903. In 1905, the red uniform was altered to the new clothing regulations. In November 1911, the Regiment participated in the coronation ceremonies of king and queen of Britain.

China (1914) and Return to India

The Regiment reached Tientsin on 28 May relieving 124th Baluchis. It did guard duties at Peking. Then it moved to form part of the British Expeditionary Force at Tsing Tao, which forced the garrison to surrender on 27 October 1914, earning the unit the Battle Honour of Tsing Tao. On 30 December, the Regiment moved to Hong Kong, and then to Jehlum, India, and formed part of 1st Infantry Brigade, tasked to deal with the Mohammands at Hafiz Khor. The task was done with finesse.

The First World War

The Regiment travelled by sea to reach Basra on 25 February 1916, forming part of 37th Brigade of the 3rd Lahore Division. It was deployed along the River Tigris carrying out numerous operational tasks. Then the Regiment marched through the marshes to drive in the Turkish positions, suffered casualties in the tune of 186 out of a strength of 650 rifles. The Turkish counter-attack was beaten back. The Regiment was bestowed with the Theatre Honour 'Mesopotamia'. On 13/14 December, in a flanking move, the Regiment was directed towards the River Hai. 36th and 45th Sikhs launched attacks together side by side, in waves, and suffered heavy casualties but captured the objective against very stiff opposition. The enemy's counter attack was beaten back. 36 Sikhs suffered 83 per cent casualties. 'Hai' was conferred as a Battle Honour to both the gallant Regiments.

The Regiment moved to Amara on 23 February 1917, and held defences on both sides of the River Tigris. Deficiencies in manpower were made up from 10th Jats, thus it now had a company of Jats. This composition remained till 1922. The Regiment thereafter moved fast by lorries and train via Ruz (rail H), Karmanshah to Hamadan, walking 283 miles. Here the task was to deal with grain and forage contractors which was done with finesse. At Manzil, it undertook operations against the Jangalis. The Regiment moved by road, then by ship from Bagdad to Amara to Busra and back to India.

Period 1919 to 1940

On 15 October 1919, the Regiment arrived at Karachi, then moved by train to Bareilly. During the period 1914 to 1921, it had suffered casualties amounting to 17 British Officers and 1026 Indians. It was conferred with several awards and Battle Honours.

In September 1920, the Regiment moved to Nowshera and carried out escort duties with the Chitral Reliefs, the third time in twenty years. It also participated in operations at Saidgi and Bannu. In mid-1921, the Jats were replaced by Punjabi Musalmans. The Battalion which was doing duty as Training Battalion was changed to an active Battalion and 35 Sikhs became the Training Battalion. The Regiment was reorganized into two companies each of Sikhs and Punjabi Musalmans. In 1928, the Regiment was changed to three companies of Sikhs and one company of Muslims, which remained till October 1947. In 1922, the Regiment became the 4th Battalion of the 11th Sikh Regiment, comprising of six Sikh units. On 11 March 1922, new Colours were received.

The Battalion moved to Ahmednagar on 13 March 1922. In 1924, the Battalion band, under Jemadar (present designation Naib Subedar) Gulab Singh, participated in the British Empire Exhibition at Wembley, coming out with flying colours.

The Unit was stationed at Aden from 1926 to 28 with detachments at two islands Perim and Kamaran. On 21 December 1927, it embarked for India, moving to Peshawar. In reorganization in 1929, a Machine Gun Company replaced the rifle company. On disturbances at Peshawar, the CO was placed in command of the City Disturbance Force, to deal with Mohamands and Afridis. All Sikh Battalions were at Peshawar: 1st (Nowshera Brigade) 2nd (Peshawar Brigade), 3rd (Jhansi Brigade) and 4th (Peshawar Brigade), at the same time. On 04 December 1931, the Battalion moved to Manzai and Wana. On 10 June 1932, Maj Gen W E Wilson Johnson, CB, CIE, DSO, was appointed Colonel of the Regiment. The Unit won all sports and professional competitions in the Wana Brigade.

The Battalion moved to Aurangabad on 21 November 1933. On 12 September 1935, while celebrating Saragarhi day, the Battalion was moved to Nowshera against the Mohamands. The Jubilee Celebrations were held at Mardan from 04 to 08 April. About 350 pensioners attended the event. A number of awards were bestowed upon the Unit personnel. The Unit was placed at Landi Kotal in 1939-40. It was then moved to Delhi, providing guards to the Viceroy and C-in-C. In June 1940, the Battalion moved to Poona to join the 7th Indian Brigade.

The Second World War

The Battalion embarked for Egypt. Enroute, the Italians bombed the flotilla of 44 ships at Massawa with a single aircraft but without much damage. On 11 October, the Battalion moved to Mena Camp, West of Cairo, joining the 7th Indian Infantry Brigade. Here, Bren Light Machine Guns, 2 and 3 inch mortars were issued. The Battalion moved to Mersa Matruh where it faced acute shortage of water. Thousands of Prisoners of War were taken by the Division. After the victory at Sidi Barrani, the Battalion moved towards Sudan and to the port of Alexandria. The Battalion as part of the Brigade covered an area of 400 miles. The Unit then joined 'Gazella Force' at Kassala which it captured. They attacked Kern Gorge where the Italians gave a good fight but were defeated when the 5th Indian Division made a threatening move to the enemy's rear. The Battalion captured Agordat after quite a to and fro battle. It then moved to Karen. Attacks continued till it was captured. Moving up ammunition and other materials was a nightmare. The Unit was then given the task of capturing Samana Ridge (a reminder of 1897 days). It was quite a battle, the battalion inflicting many more casualties on the enemy than it suffered. The Unit, task done they then moved back to Kassala, on to Giarabub in Egypt. The enemy bombing throughout kept the Unit on its toes. A number of sportsmen displayed their grit and sacrificed their lives. The Battalion then moved to Mersa Matru – Sidi Barrani, and onwards to Sofafi. It was a part of the attack on Amara suffering numerous casualties, but winning laurels and awards. They then had to face the German 21st Panzer Division at Sidi Rezegh. The Battalion was thereafter moved to Derna and then to Tobruk. Almost 20000 all ranks of German and Italian Armies were taken prisoner. The ferocity of the battle was such that 183 aircraft were destroyed in these battles.

The Battalion then moved to Benghazi, carrying out a number of tasks under the 4th Indian Division, then moved on to El Adem in February 1942. Relations with H M S Sikh was established. The threat to the Middle East having reached a pitch, brigades from the 4th and 5th Indian Divisions were sent to Iraq. A six day journey by train and convoy took the Battalion to Baghdad. Here memories of World War I were revived by a visit to the Church where the Battalion had earlier made some presentations. It crossed the deserts to Haifa, then returning to Cairo, Egypt, and then to Mersa Matruh. Enemy aircraft bombed the Battalion and caused several casualties. The Unit was moved to El Alamein. The Germans were following throughout. 2 Sikh provided a covering position at Mersa Matruh. Defences were dug up in the rocky area of Deir al Shein, where water was so scarce that men were rationed it to half a gallon a day. There now was a likelihood of greater intensity of the war. Feverish preparations were being made all over. Apart from the Indians, there also were South Afrikans and New Zealanders. The lines were drawn for a pitched battles at El Alamein. The battle was fought from 23 October to 04 November 1942. Tanks churned out sand all over making visibility poor. Under severe pressure, the Battalion had to vacate its positions, assembling at Hammam and then to Cairo. Losses were heavy in to tune of seven British Officers, nine Viceroy Commissioned Officers and 500 Other Ranks. The Unit was refitted for a month at Cairo. It then moved to Haifa on 12 August, where it carried out guard duties. It was under strength. It celebrated Saragarhi day here. Punjabi Musalmans visited Jerusalem. Many learnt Arabic.

After nine months at Haifa, the Battalion was moved by transport to the newly formed Mountain Warfare Training Centre at Lebanon Hills. Gruelling training was imparted. In April 1944, the Battalion moved to a hill station Slenfe in Syria. The Battalion again moved back to Haifa via Tripoli, and in July was shipped to Italy. It travelled by road and rail, through Rome, to join the 8th Army, 10th Indian Brigade on 8th August at Montorchi. The Battalion was then made part of 4th Indian Division, where 2 Sikh had already made a mark with its gallant fights. It was lifted to 5th Indian Division in its attacks on the Gothic Line, advancing to village of Monte Calvo. It launched a quick attack, surprised the enemy and inflicted numerous casualties. The Germans were forced out of the village. The Battalion captured San Marino after an extremely stiff battle and then transferred to Greece. The Battalion had suffered 300 casualties in all these actions. Stationed at Tavernelle, it enjoyed visits to Rome and Florence. The Battalion was then transferred to 10 Infantry Division towards the Lemone River, near San Marino. Winter conditions were at their severest. Plans were being constantly changed. The Battalion attacked Cassetti Farmhouse, capturing it but faced German counter attacks which were defeated. On 03 January 1945, it took a defensive position at River Senio. It then moved to Tiber Valley for rest, from there to Bologna, and to Frassineto. The Battalion was attacked with full ferocity but the enemy attack was beaten back.

The 'cease fire' was announced on 29th January 1945 when the Battalion was astride the Reno River, at the disputed territory of the Morgan Line. Here, the Unit carried out the uncomfortable duty of keeping peace between the Yugoslavs and the Italians. The Unit paid visits to Venice and parts of Austria. Some men visited UK. The Battalion was then moved to South of Milan. It moved out of Italy on the 24th. The Unit landed back at Karachi on 05 December. It further moved to the Training Centre at Nowshera and then to Campbellpur.

Period 1945 to 1962

India attained independence on 15 August 1947. Partition based on communal lines affected Bengal and Punjab, dividing the two into two halves each. Millions of people from both sides were uprooted to move to regions unknown, to begin a new life. There was mass destruction, looting, killing and rape. The composition in 4 Sikh was 50 per cent each of Sikhs and Muslims. It goes to the credit of regimentation in the Unit that no untoward incident occurred. The Unit carried out its assignments of internal security duties at Sargodha, Mianwali and Jhang. The Sikhs from Punjab units joined 4 Sikh while Punjabi Musalman from the Unit moved to Pakistan battalions. The separation was heart rending. The Battalion moved to Jalandhar and then to Ferozepur, escorting Muslim refugees via Sulaimanki and Hussainiwala.

A contingent of 330 personnel participated in the Prime Minister and Defence Minister's Ceremonial Parade at Jalandhar. The Unit then moved to Karnal for security duties. The Regimental Centre had moved to Ambala and thus was of great help. The Unit won all the formation professional as well as sports competitions, hockey taking the cake.

True to record, where there was trouble, 4 Sikh moved there, and now to Uri, J&K where woes with Pakistan had resurfaced. The operational responsibility was opposite Hajipir Pass, at Ledigali and Pir Kanthi on the Pir Panjal Range. The 'cease fire' was declared at midnight to be effective immediately. Had the Battalion been told a day or two earlier, it would have improved its defensive posture. The Defence Minister, Sardar Baldev Singh paid a visit to Uri on 12 April 1949. A Guard of Honour was presented to the PM at Srinagar. Many dignitaries visited the Unit. It also continued to excel in all professional as well as sports competitions. While doing training at Achhabal Camp, it made a pilgrimage to Amarnath Caves; going and coming in record time. Saragarhi Day was celebrated at Mughal Gardens, attended by a host of dignitaries.

Regimental/King's Colours, presented at Nowshera, were laid at NDA Dehradun on 23 November 1950. The Battalion was moved to Alwar in December 1950 to join 163 Infantry Brigade, commanded by the Unit's first Indian CO. End June 1951, Pakistan again started making noises. 4 Sikh was again assigned to occupy defences opposite Hajipir Pass. Saragarhi Day was celebrated in spite of the din. The Battalion carried out a number of flag marches in Northern Ladakh, besides its own operational responsibilities. Two IAS Probationer groups were attached with the Unit at different times. It goes to the credit of its overall performance, and also to the satisfaction of the UNO officers that in appreciation they presented a UNO Flag, perhaps for the first and last time in its history along the Indo-Pak LOC. The Unit moved to Mehander, and then to Ranchi. Thereafter, the Unit moved to Ramgarh.

Indo-China War 1962: Battle of Walong

The Unit was celebrating Saragarhi Day when the orders were received to move to Walong. OIC Advance Party sent a message 'Favourable terrain to enact another Saragarhi'. The Unit detrained at Jorhat and from there airlifted in Otters (capacity one section of 10 men) in a number of sorties over a number of days to its operational area. Meanwhile, the Chinese had attacked 6 Kumaon forward positions and pushed them back. Initial positions of 4 Sikh were two companies at Kibithoo and one each at Walong and Teju, to be changed to two companies each astride the River Lohit. The heights ranged between 5 to 8000 feet. The ground was hard, digging extremely difficult, water was scarce which along with food, ammunition and war requirements had to be brought up, by a six hours gruelling walk. On night 20/21 October, the Chinese launched attacks across the Mac Mahon Line. They pushed back 6 Kumaon screen position at Ashi Hill, followed the Kumaonis, to be stopped by 'B' Company of 4 Sikh at Mithun Track/Maha Plateau. Many were killed and returned burning the dry grass all around. There was a terrible stench because of Chinese dead bodies. One company of 2/8 GR married up with 4 Sikh. Due to repeated defeats of the Chinese they were frustrated and named the 4 Sikh positions as 'Tiger Mouth'. Reorganization of the defences was ordered, 4 Sikh to occupy West Bank and 6 Kumaon to defend the East Bank, however, it could not be implanted due to the enemy's persistent attacks, and 'A', 'C' and 'B' companies continued on the West Bank and 'D' company on the East bank. A Company of 2/8 GR was also on the West Bank. All positions in depth were held by 6 Kumaon. On 27 October, Brig J C Hartley took over the Brigade. Lt Gen Harbaksh Singh Vr C, the Corps Commander visited the location. Patrolling and ambush clashes were a constant feature. On 14 November, 6 Kumaon attacked Yellow Pimple but were beaten back suffering many casualties. 4 Dogra was inducted and took positions at Tri Junction.

The Chinese main attack came on 15/16 November on East Bank. They were spotted crossing Lohit River in rubber boats. They attacked High Plateau ('D' Company) and pressure increased at Patrol Base ('A' Company). Attacks in waves were launched. While this was going on, it was seen that the heavy battery behind 'B' Company positions withdrew. 4 Sikh had no such orders. The troops of 3/3 GR also withdrew through 4 Sikh Battalion Headquarters. The situation by 10.45 am was critical, the Chinese overlooking 4 Sikh positions. Walong was shelled heavily. Final orders to withdraw were received at 1.30pm on 16 November. 4 Sikh withdrew after resisting persistent attacks for 25 days continuously, a longest period anywhere in the 1962 war.

4 Sikh suffered 82 killed and 97 wounded, while 2 officers, 2 RO and 40 ORs were taken PoW since they could not move back being wounded. Out of four company commanders, two had died fighting, one was wounded and taken a PoW.

December 1962 to September 1965

The Unit was stationed at Lekhapani, Tirap Division. To erase the memory of the 1962 debacle, revamp of the Battalion was carried out in an exceptionally mature manner. HH Lt Gen Yadvidra Singh of Patiala visited the Unit. The Unit had made its own bamboo hutment village which was the envy of the Station and the locals. Many sportsmen represented Command and Services. In the shooting competition the Unit stood first in the Division. The Unit, moved to Kameng Division. It was stationed at Rupa with a task along the Bhutan borders. New pre-fabricated accommodation was built here. The Unit excelled in every sphere of military activity. Admiral B S Soman, the Chief of Naval Staff, visited the Unit. In July 1965, the Unit was moved to a well-deserved peace station – Ferozepur, after three and a half years continuous service in the East, including fighting the war.

Indo-Pak War 1965

True to tradition, the Battalion moved to a peace station when the rumours of war were in the air. Reaching Ferozepur in the month of August, the Unit got into celebration mode of Saragarhi Day, yet preparing for imminent war. On 03 September, the Unit was placed on four hour notice for a task in an undisclosed location. The Battalion was moved to Khalra on Bhikhiwind-Barki-Lahore axis. On 06 September, the Unit was the first to cross the International Border, capturing two enemy Border Outposts Rakh Hardit Singh and Theh Sarja Marja, providing a corridor to another Infantry Brigade to capture Barki by the evening. But the Brigade was held up at Hudiara Drain, the Unit's Infantry Brigade taking the move forward, on the 8th, with 4 Sikh leading. It captured Brahmnabad and cleared the area towards Barka Kalan. 9 Madras secured Barka Kalan and 16 Punjab Barka Khurad, two villages astride the road. On night 10/11 September, 4 Sikh launched a night attack to capture Barki, a formidable defensive position held by two companies plus Ichhogil Canal in its rear. After an extremely stiff opposition based on pillboxes and bombing to the tune of 3000 rounds to beat back the attack, the Battalion captured not only Barki but exploited to include the Phase 2 objective of the Brigade, capture of Ichhogil by 16 Punjab. The enemy commander was awarded Pakistans highest gallantry award of 'Nishan E Haider'. 4 Sikh 'A' and 'C' Companies captured Barki village East of the road and 'D' the Police Station area West of the road. 'B' Company moved forward for reorganization phase.

The Battalion had 39 killed and 121 wounded. Battle Honour 'Barki' and Theatre Honour 'Punjab' were conferred on the Battalion. There were many whose gallantry went unnoticed since the Battalion was assigned an ill planned task the very next day.

On 11 September, in spite of numerous casualties, being six days continuously in battle, the Battalion was given an ill-conceived task without adequate intelligence and reconnaissance, in another sector, under a different formation at Khemkaran on the axis to Kasur. The Unit established the road block on the road to Kasur behind Khemkaran, but the Division was unable to establish a link up. As a result, the Unit was encircled by enemy armour in large numbers, against which the Unit had no effective defence mechanism. The CO, four officers and 120 ORs were surrounded in small groups in a spread out area of three kilometers and captured. The personnel were kept at Lahore, Kohat and Dargai, to be repatriated in

February 1966, after five months captivity. (The author was also taken as PoW).

The Unit was moved back to Barki where the President of India, Dr Radha Krishnan visited and highly appreciated the gallant deeds and numerous sacrifices made.

1965 to 1971

In February 1966, the personnel who had been repatriated were reinstalled in the Unit. The Battalion then moved to Poonch where it was deployed on the highest posts of Point 405. It excelled in all competitions the brigade and division. The Battalion, along with other units of the Sikh Regiment were presented new Colours by the President of India at the Regimental Centre at Meerut. Completing its field tenure, it moved to Ramgarh. On likelihood of impending operations in the East, the Unit was moved to Phulia and, poised for Bayora border. Intense training was carried out to prepare for the war.

Indo-Pak War 1971

East Bengal, now Bangladesh, is a country of rivers, streams and marshes. The country side was nothing but swamps in the rainy season. There were few metalled roads and the houses were mostly *'katcha'* mud houses with thatched roofs. There was thick foliage all around. The terrain blended itself to defensive operations and was a nightmare for offensive actions requiring intense planning and preparations. The Battalion crossed the border on 10 November 1971, and advanced to clear and hold Makapur, Hijuli, Ballabhpur and Naodapara. On 20 Nov, the Battalion carried out deep penetration, advancing with speed, against devastating enemy fire and secured the Western bank of Kabadhak River at Chaugacha. The enemy's counter attack which had taken a bite of the Eastern portion of the Bandh was evacuated with a quick counter attack by our own troops supported by tanks. On 21 November, the Battalion crossed the river in country boats and secured Chaugacha, a hub well defended, an enormous amount of weapon and stores were recovered.

There were many to and fro moves. Burinda on the outskirts of Jessore was attacked with two of our battalions which were repulsed with heavy casualties. The task was then entrusted to 4 Sikh who with a stealthy move by one Company bit into a limb of the enemy defences on an elongated

Bandh reinforced by solid bunkers well stocked with ample ammunition. Thereafter, the Battalion cleared the entire Bandh, bit by bit. The enemy evacuated Jessore which was found to be abandoned when our troops moved in on 07 December. A number of units had undertaken bold actions along with armour, and artillery doing a magnificent task and the sappers taking massive tasks of road building and laying of bridges.

The enemy 107 Infantry Brigade then abandoned its forward positions and withdrew to Khulna, which was approachable only from one side and was defended by almost four infantry battalions with the fifth reserve in Khulna itself. 9 Infantry Division hammered the enemy in every possible way on the only approach available, yet the enemy held its own inflicting some severe casualties on our forces. A special task was then assigned to 4 Sikh to attack the rear cutting through defences of enemy three battalions, 1500 metres depth, to establish a road block on the only artery available to the enemy to sustain its forces. The attack was launched company by company due to depth of the objective area. Establishment of the road block was successful. The enemy had been cut off, own casualties were considerable. Brigadier Hayat Khan, Commander 107 Infantry Brigade surrendered at the road block site by 10am. The honour to enter Khulna leading the victory march was given to 4 Sikh, leading company mounted on tanks, under shouts of *'Joy Bangla'*.

In these operations the Unit suffered killed 38; wounded 06 officers, 06 JCOs, 155 ORs and 02 NCEs. The Unit was bestowed with Battle Honour 'Siramani'.

Period 1972 to 1987

The Unit was pulled out from Bangladesh on 22 December 1971 and was moved back to Ramgarh. Hundreds of Pak PoW had been kept there. They were creating a lot of problems for the units, especially PoW officers. This difficult and tricky duty was given to 4 Sikh. A number of bids by Pak PoW to escape were foiled by the alert Sikhs in a very hostile atmosphere of heat, dust storms and terrible cold. Captain A C B Wimbush, Signal Platoon Commander during Second World War visited the Unit in November 1973.

On 18 December 1973, the Battalion moved to Missamari. The Unit was further moved to Mizoram where the insurgency problem had escalated. The Unit was split into Companies and Platoons along the long stretch of road from Aizawl to Lungle, providing security, besides undertaking special missions to apprehend hostile elements. The counter insurgency task was well performed for five months, 4 Sikh moved back to Missamari on 25 May 1975. It had apprehended 14 hard core insurgents along with host of weapons and ammunition. The Unit moved to Ranchi on 21 July 1976. Saragarhi Day had a special significance when Subedar Nahar Singh told his stories of participation in the Battles of Tsing Tao (1914), Kut-Et-Mara (1916) and Italy (1917). In June 1979, the Battalion was rushed by air to Bhubneshwar to carry out a very delicate and risky task of disarming two CRPF battalions.

The Unit moved to Pallanwala-Jaurian on 27 March 1980, and to Ferozepur on 23 February 1983. In spite of being located in a very volatile situation in 1984, it goes to the credit of the discipline of the Unit and an excellent control by the CO, officers and JCOs that not a single untoward incident occurred. Silver Jubilee of Battle of Barki was celebrated with elan.

The Unit moved to Pathankot by road on 09 May 1986. It was part of 51 Infantry Brigade. This station had been selected by Lieutenant General P S Vadehra to celebrate the Raising Day Centenary. The Unit was allotted an undeveloped area. Besides operational and training responsibilities a number of projects were undertaken to get the area developed, especially the Officers Mess, JCOs Mess and Battalion Gurudwara. Numerous schemes were undertaken, all the institutes were given an incredible make over, many articles of use were renovated or purchased anew, yellow chevrons of the NCO's were reinstated, Unit's own tie and scarf were restarted after decades, an impressive mobile memorial was created, a book on the history of the Unit was released and an iconic painting was made. The celebrations were marked with a record number of erstwhile officers, JCOs and men of the Unit and Regiment, including from the UK, attending the celebrations. The highlights in which a large number of guests participated were a ceremonial parade led by the Commanding Officer, an exhibition in massive igloos and a highly spirited 'Barakhana'.

The Unit then moved from Chakki Bank railway station to Rupa in Arunachal on 17 May 1989, to join 311 Mountain Brigade. It was in the same area where it had served in 1964-65. It was nostalgic to be around the Saragarhi stadium which had been established way back. 4 Sikh continued its winning streak in competitions, training, mobilization and operational responsibilities. It was especially deployed in Nazira, Sibsagar and Simalguri areas of Assam to deal with ULFA insurgency where it did a commendable job.

It moved to Sriganganagar on 03 May 1991, from the high hills of Arunachal to riverine and jungle terrain of Assam and then to deserts, adapting to every situation. It was part of 15 Infantry Brigade. Here, it had to move to the borders for operational rehearsals in anti-infiltration mode. The Unit was put through a number of exercises.

Starting on 25 July 1994, the Unit reached its next field station at Uri in J&K, on the orbat of 12 Infantry Brigade. The unit was in defence and anti-infiltration role on the East of River Jehlum, occupying Baaz Battalion area. The Unit outwitted infiltration bids by adopting sound measures, with developed sources and good liaison with the locals of many villages in the area.

In December 1996 it moved to Ferozepur. It joined 65 Infantry Brigade, on whose orbat, it had captured Barki in 1965. The place was especially chosen to celebrate the Centenary of Battle of Saragarhi, since Saragarhi Memorial Gurudwara was located there. Besides participation in all formation and station duties, the Unit carried out preparations for the great day in a very methodical and efficient manner. Numerous functions for three days were organized including a ceremonial parade, led by the Commanding Officer and a State function at the Memorial Gurudwara, addressed by the then Chief Minister of Punjab, Sardar Prakash Singh Badal. Numerous dignitaries, both from Army and Civil graced the several functions.

Once again, the Unit moved to Kupwara, J&K, this time in the Balbir-Pathra area of 268 Infantry Brigade. It was deployed in an extremely rugged hilly and high altitude area, against a treacherous enemy who kept the Unit personnel engaged in firing and infiltration. It was quite a trying time. The Unit had an upper hand along the border and also eliminated or apprehended many infiltrators during the period of its stay there from October 1999 to December 2001.

The Unit thereafter moved to Rajasthan for its peacetime tenure. It was part of 167 Infantry Brigade. It got tuned to deserts in no time and took on the operational responsibility in Operation PARAKARAM adroitly. Emphasis was on mobilization, defensive/offensive tasks, IS duties and professional and sports competitions. Remaining part of the same formation, the Unit was moved to Lucknow, where it was stationed from October 2002 to November 2004.

4 Sikh moved to Dalapchand (Kalimpong) in November 2004. It had the operational task at the high altitude area at Saragarhi complex along the Indo-China border up to September 2005.

UN Mission to Lebanon

It was on 03 September, the Unit moved from Bagdogra to Delhi. It was located at Khanpur Camp for training and preparation for a move to Lebanon on UN Mission as peacemakers. It moved by air to Lebanon on 07 December 2005. It took over responsibilities along the border between Israel and Lebanon. Numerous presentations were carried out to understand the countries involved, and operations that had already taken place. The Force Commander, UNIFIL visited frequently at HQ INDBATT VIII, 4 Sikh location at Naqur Kawkaba. Adequate care was taken for hundreds of mines laid in the area earlier. Marches for peace and harmony were conducted and good relationship with locals and contingents from several other countries was established. Each and every violation from either side was meticulously reported to higher headquarters, including hundreds of all types of munitions fired by the Israelis. The Unit personnel, deployed at 19 posts, spread out for several kilometers. XXXVI withstood the 34 days war, 12 July to 14 August, during which Israel Defence Forces fired 40,000 artillery bombs, 800 aerial bombs, 5,000 tank rounds, 1,150 Katyusha rockets and thousands of small arms rounds, 87 munitions fell close to our own positions. The Unit, for its resolute and courageous devotion to duty was awarded the 'Unit Citation' and 81 Commendation Cards. Besides numerous visits and accolades by international dignitaries, the singular honour was the visit of UN Secretary General, Mr Kofi Annan, the first time to any unit on UN Mission till then.

XXXVI proved its record of participating in all the wars at Lebanon, on a mission to keep peace. The spirit inculcated by the Battle of Saragarhi provided enough fodder for grit and determination. The Battalion landed back at Delhi on 04 January 2007. On 13 March 2007, it moved to Mamun Cantonment, Pathankot, under 90 Infantry Brigade of 9 Infantry Division. It performed well in all operational oriented, professional and sports competitions, and was adjudged the best Battalion, having been awarded the 'Gurj Division Sports Banner', and 'Overall Champion Trophy'.

Highest Battlefield

The Unit moved out on 16 August 2010 for its turn to High Altitude responsibility, to the highest battlefield of the world, Siachen. It got its training and did systematic acclimatization at Base Camp, and then took over tasks on the Central Glacier. Due to extreme cold and high altitude to the tune of 15,000 to 21,000 feet, deployed from 09 October 2010 to 26 August 2011, the Unit had its share of some casualties due to mines, engagements with the enemy and physical inconveniences. It was found to be apt in patrolling, track maintenance, route-opening, and construction of helipads. The Units efforts to improve habitat were colossal, which included putting up Russian tents, ice caves and use of snow scooters. From August 2011 to August 2012, the Unit was located at Fukche for Leh – Ladakh vigil, along the borders. The overall performance of the Unit was highly applauded by all commanders in the chain, especially COAS. The Battalion was bestowed with several awards.

2012 – Till Date

The Unit moved to its deserving peace tenure at Chandimandir Cantonment in August 2012. A peace station, but the operational and station duties next to the Command Headquarters kept the Unit busy. The visits of dignitaries were numerous professional and sports competitions unending, participation in regimental and civil relationship interminable, and yet preparation and readiness for the operational tasks was of utmost priority. All this done superbly was evident from the ultimate award of the coveted 'GOC-in-C Western Command Unit Citation' on 15 January 2015.

On 25 September 2015, XXXVI moved to Arunachal Pradesh, at Lekhapani as rear and deployment for Longding Battalion Area of Responsibility. It was nostalgic to be at Lekhapani, where the Unit was stationed after the 1962 Indo-Pak War. It had the dual responsibility; in counter insurgency role and defense along the Indo-China Border. For CI mission, the pre-induction training was completed at Vairangte, the Unit was given responsibility of an area of 82 by 20 square kilometers. The area had an international border with Mayanmar of 7.5 kilometers. The insurgents to be dealt with were all sections of NSCN and ULFA cadres, in a treacherous and mountainous terrain. The tasks involved military and psychological operations, civic and socio-political actions, all done with aplomb to the appreciation of all. The Unit was instrumental in apprehending 40 insurgents, 20 weapons and abundance of ammunition and cash. For the conventional role, many exercises, long range patrols and constant vigil was kept along the borders and in the area of responsibility.

The Unit then moved to Bathinda in Punjab, by the end of August 2018.

It would thus be found that in its entire existence, especially after the Battle of Saragarhi, 4 Sikh's (XXXVI's) indomitable spirits have soared high. Wherever it has served, fortunately in almost all wars, battles and insurgencies it has brought unlimited credit. Its adaption to snow clad mountains in high altitude areas, rugged mountains, thick jungles and riverine terrain, scorching deserts, in India or far-flung countries; it has proved its metal. Its service to uphold its traditions of bravery, courage, devotion to duty and sacrifice in service to the Indian Nishan 'The Tricolour' has been constant. In whatever conditions, it has always celebrated the Saragarhi Day in the best possible manner, the beacon always upheld.

CHAPTER FOURTEEN

RECOGNITION: EPILOGUE: FUTURE TRENDS

"A people which takes no pride in the noble achievements of remote ancestors, will never achieve anything worthy to be remembered with pride of remote descendents."

– Macaulay

General

This then is the saga of extreme bravery. Since the occurrence of the event at Saragarhi, to commemorate the ultimate sacrifice, a great deal has been done by the Governments, military and individuals at various places. However, there is always scope for turning the pages of history further, to bring out minute detail – informative, educative and emulative – in a way not done in the past and make the account of Saragarhi our heritage and inspiration for generations to come.

Every generation needs its own inspirational connection, acts that instill perseverance and resolve, and lay claim on it not only by a segment of the populace but the entire country. It must touch the national psyche in the way of national icon and inheritance. The Battle of Saragarhi meets this need.

What we already have

The news of the supreme bravery at Saragarhi spread all over like wild fire. Accolades and glowing tributes started pouring in. The British Parliament in England learnt of the news when in session. In an instant reaction, all arose giving a standing ovation.

Using the stones of the ruined post at Saragarhi, the Government erected a Cairn at the Site on 20 September 1897. The Cairn lies fallen today with time, lack of upkeep and an earthquake in 1971.

Regarding the plaque on the obelisk, an interesting story often told is that when Pakistan was in the process of assimilating the Orakazai country, someone proposed the removal of the stone on it since it eulogized the bravery of the Sikhs, who were not any braver than the Pathans who attacked them. The reply was convincing enough for the stone to stay, "Let it stand, for if these Sikhs had not been there you would probably be part of Afghanistan today."

Another testimony of the acts of the Government was the erection of a Memorial at Fort Lockhart, which still stands proud. The recognition by the United Nations Organization (UNO) of this battle as one of the bravest made it famous internationally. France and Germany took it upon themselves to include the incident of valour in the curriculum of their schools.

In the same vein of appropriate acts of recognition and acceptance of the bravest episode and uniqueness of the battle, the British Government erected a Saragarhi Gurudawara at Amritsar on 14 February 1902, on the way to the Golden Temple. The area had become an eye sore because of mushrooming of all sorts of mini shops and vendors, as many encroached upon the land around the Gurudawara. The Government of Punjab, under the Chief Minister Parkash Singh Badal, with its gigantic efforts in 2015-17 have removed all that was ugly and given a spectacular glory to the Gurudawara, making it a part of a grand plaza leading to Harmandir Sahib. The Management of the holy shrine has further enhanced the façade and grandeur by constructing a magnificent Saragarhi Sarai (inn) behind the Saragarhi Gurudawara.

The newspaper 'Pioneer' raised funds and distributed it to the families of the martyrs of Saragarhi. It further got a Memorial Gurudawara made at Ferozepur, this place was selected since maximum martyrs belonged to the area. The Memorial was dedicated to the Public by Sir Charles Pevz, the Governor of Punjab in 1904.

The British Government awarded posthumous IOMs, the then highest award given to Indian soldiers, to all the martyred soldiers, ironically the non-combatant was omitted though as deserving. The Government also granted Rupees 500 as reward and two '*murabbas*' (equal to 25 acres) of land to the descendants of each of the martyrs. 12 September was declared to be observed as a Regimental holiday, in perpetuity, for all regiments enlisting Sikhs. 'Saragarhi' was granted as a 'Battle Honour' for the Sikh Regiment. In March 1900, a G.G.O. (No 16) was issued authorizing the Regiment to bear upon its Colours and Appointment, the honorary distinctions specified below in commemoration of its gallant conduct and distinguished service during the operations on the North-West Frontier in 1897-1898:

(a) PUNJAB FRONTIER
(b) SAMANA
(c) TIRAH

A Memorial was built at the Sikh Regimental Center at Meerut when Major General V R Khanolkar was the Colonel of the Regiment and Lieutenant Colonel Budh Singh was the Commandant of the Centre. Another Memorial was raised at the new Regimental Centre at Ramgarh in December 1991, an initiative of the author as Commandant. The Memorial was inaugurated by Lieutenant General P S Vadehra, PVSM, in 1992. The Memorial today has an imposing 'Motivation and Museum Hall' behind it, another initiative of the author. Its foundation was laid on 09 October 1993 and was inaugurated by Lt Gen M S Bhullar, PVSM, SM on 02 May 1955 when Col T S Kalra was the Commandant. The author had also got a mobile Memorial made in 4 Sikh in 1987 and restarted its tie and scarf in red and yellow colours after a gap of almost forty years, in keeping up with the colours of its ceremonials at the time of its raising in 1887. The first ever book on a Unit's history 'Ashes to Glory – The Saragarhi Battalion', eulogizing the Battle of Saragarhi was also published by the author when he was the Commanding Officer of the Unit on its Centenary.

The newly built War Punjab State Heroes Memorial and Museum at Amritsar, inaugurated on 23 October 2016, by Sardar Parkash Singh Badal, ex-CM Punjab on the road to the Wagha Border depicts the battle in a large panorama. There are some informative artifacts placed inside the Museum.

The descendants and villagers of Havildar Ishar Singh and Naik Lal Singh have constructed memorials in their villages out of their own contributions where they congregate every year to commemorate their valiant predecessors. There was a presentation by Lieutenant General K S Randhawa PVSM, AVSM, on 11 September 2007 at Delhi, where he narrated details of his visit to the site and showed the latest photographs.

Captain Amarinder Singh, the Chief Minister of Punjab has written a detailed book "Saragarhi and the Defence of the Samana Forts – The 36th Sikhs in the Tirah Campaign 1897-98" in 2017, on the 120th Commemoration of the Battle of Saragarhi. The Memorial Gurudawara at Ferozepur, a defence property, had almost been handed over to a religious sect when Captain A S Jaijee of 4 Sikh raised the issue with the Chief Minister, who promptly ordered the restoration of the Memorial to a Trust. His Government has taken sterling steps to accept a long standing request of the Sikh Regiment and the 'Saragarhi Memorials and Ethos Promotion Forum' established by the veterans of the Sikh Regiment, to include the battle in the curriculum of schools in Punjab. (The author is one of the founding members of the 'Forum' and now one of the trustees of a 'Trust' established by the Captain Amarinder Singh's Government to manage the affairs of the Ferozepur Memorial Gurudawara).

Captain Amarinder Singh, the CM, and his Cabinet have taken another most befitting step to declare 12 September a holiday in Punjab. After decades of ignored State function at Ferozepur that one time used to be the norm, the CM has restarted the same in a dignified mode. His laudable approach to the pious spot where the battle of Saragarhi was fought has resulted in two fallen stones which formed the fort walls, to be brought to India, and presented by him as preserves to the Sikh Regimental Centre and 4 Sikh (XXXVI) on Vaisakhi Day 2018. His continuous efforts have ultimately established the presence, sacrifice and whereabouts of the brave martyr NCE Karmdaad, – details given earlier.

Many highly appreciative appropriate steps and initiatives have been taken in India as well as in UK, USA and Australia to establish memorable artifacts and memorials besides written material. Mister Gurinderpal Singh Josan, a research scholar, based in USA, published his book "The Saga of Valour – The Epic Battle of Saragarhi" in 2014, whose Second Edition, has been released in September 2017, coinciding with the Commemoration of the 120th celebrations of this magnificent battle. Another gentleman from UK, Mr Jay Singh Sohal has organized presentations of the battle at Delhi and Sandhurst, UK.

Some movie and documentary producers have also stepped in to generate pictures and videos of the iconic battle. Some stories, due to lack of accurate information or due to haste have been garbled, yet the basis of enterprise to present bravery at its best has been retained and well showcased.

What Next?

The war memorials are befitting edifices which remind us of the valour and sacrifices of our ancestors, but true memorials have to be imbibed in the hearts for which some added efforts have been taken by the Punjab Government. Rightly, a different approach is the demand of the day. To this end, well researched books are the ultimate. The documentaries and comics due to lack of accuracies reflect a questionable presentation. The movies and documentaries are also liable to bring in inaccuracies, especially due to pressing reasons of a commercial perspective. They need to have technical advisors who know the subject.

It needs to be appreciated that history needs to have a personal appeal to be relevant. The aspect of creating memories in the minds and hearts of the people must get its due importance. The memories after all, become inspirations at the time of crisis, which needs to be inculcated especially in young minds.

Therefore, there is a need to analyze how public conscience can be stimulated so that future generations are motivated and inspired in martial courage and determination.

Memorials and areas around these must be made spectacularly presentable. Any and everybody erecting a memorial for a single martyr should not be encouraged, especially for every sacrificial death. In fact it is desirable to define a martyr in its true sense. Every soldier dying, though on duty, should not necessarily be projected and accepted as a martyr. Solemnity and dignity must be maintained by erecting memorials on a selective basis where a number of names of the martyrs are solemnized; this of course is different to national or state level memorials. Spaces can be marked where busts of martyrs can be added. The whole space is thus created into a strikingly presentable structure, soliciting spontaneous veneration, where not only bigger functions can be held but also become attractive to tourists. In case of necessity of historical, social or situational commemoration at a lesser level, the same can also be carried out at specified restricted areas at places suitably. If such memorials have a museum close by it will add to the attraction, also providing authentic information. Mushrooming of small memorials, made in a hurry, often have problems of maintenance and management. In many a case, even proper architectural advice from experts has not been taken.

The books written so far or in the offing should automatically become the concern of the Governments (National or State level). Suitable ones should be recommended to various libraries, for the study of the public in general. A selection committee can be formed to choose suitable books which could be recommended to other States. The event of Saragarhi should find a place in the books of almost all the States, as it is an unparalleled epic of chivalry, patriotism, sacrifice and camaraderie.

The 'Light and Sound' programmes of the highest order should be enacted at selected places – to name a few Delhi, Lucknow, Jaipur, Ferozepur, Amritsar, Jhansi, Patna, Mumbai and selected academies. (The Punjab Government has already taken an initiative).

An institute of international significance needs to be made on Saragarhi, viz; a defence institute, an aerodrome, a university or a high tech medical facility. A thought may be given to creating a Saragarhi Chair in universities, having history as a subject.

AN ODE

By Ganeev Kaur Dhillon, Class 12, Carmel Convent School, Chandigarh

"A tale be told, long forgotten, brought forth from the memories of the old.

Of 21 men who, died at duty's call, who laid down their lives, and let not the fort fall.

Twas the year 1897, the battle of Saragarhi was waged, 10,000 Afghans, 21 Sikhs yet for hours the battle raged.

Outnumbered and surrounded, and still the men fought on, with a stubbornness and pride for which, the Sikhs have long been known.

Charge after charge was repulsed, and nary a bullet was wasted, and though the battle was lost, it was victory that the men tasted.

Now, the defenders ranks were dwindling, and the ammunition would soon be over. The wall was breached; the gate was rushed, it was the final hour.

Hand-to-hand fighting followed, and the men fell one by one, and each took 'sawa lakh' with him, before he was done.

A handful of men, a fort of stones, mud walls and a wooden door, but when the last man had fallen, at least 600 of the enemy were dead, the wounded many more.

Under Havildar Ishar Singh, they fought to the last man, last breath, they had promised their all to the motherland, and fulfilled their all with their death.

And the world stood up to honour, the heroic deed of 21 men, that challenged the annals of history, to tell of more glorious action, if it can.

Today we forget our history, as we sway to foreign music and dance, while they teach the battle of Saragarhi, to the students in far off France.

And we know not the men of Saragarhi, while the UNESCO includes their tale, in the 5 most significant events of its kind, collective bravery on the highest of scale.

And we remember not the men of Saragarhi, the men who took a stand, and we care not for the men of Saragarhi, who laid down their lives for our land."

> "Recounting Battle of Saragarhi, the ultimate supreme epitome of steadfastness, chivalry and sacrifice, germinates a kind of exhilaration. The nostalgic images of the 'grime and shine' take form - ravishing, peerless, pulsating and memorable. The memoirs, memorials and enactments of 'daring and dauntless' inspire to emanate. The glorious past rekindles an innate spirit to recreate the 'hallowed' attainment of patriotism and to live and sacrifice for the truth and pious beliefs."
>
> – **Brigadier Kanwaljit Singh Veteran**

APPENDICES

Appendix A
(Refers to Chapter One)

Durand Line Agreement
(November 12, 1893)

Agreement between Amir Abdur Rahman Khan. G. C. S. I.., and Sir Henry Mortimer Durand. K. C. I. E., C. S. I.

Whereas certain questions have arisen regarding the frontier of Afghanistan on the side of India are desirous of settling these questions by friendly understanding, so that for the future there may be no difference of opinion on the subject between the allied Governments, it is hereby agreed as follows:

1. The eastern and southern frontier of his highness's dominions, from Wakhan to the Persian border, shall follow the line shown in the map attached to his agreement.
2. The Government of India will at no time exercise interference in the territories lying beyond this line on the side of Afghanistan, and his Highness the Amir will at no time exercise interference in the territories lying beyond this line on the side of India.
3. The British Government thus agrees to His Highness the Amir retaining Asmar and the valley above it, as far as Chanak. His Highness agrees, on the other hand, that he will at no time exercise interference in Swat, Bajaur, or Chitral, including the Arnawai or Bashgal valley. The British Government also agrees to leave to His Highness, who relinquishes his claim to the rest of the Waziri country and Dawar. His Highness also relinquishes his claim to Chageh.
4. The frontier line will hereafter be laid down in detail and demarcated, wherever this may be particable and desirable, by joint British and Afghan commissioners, whose object will be to arrive by mutual understanding at a boundary which shall adhere with the greatest possible exactness to the line shown in the map attached to tis agreement, having due regards to the existing local rights of villages adjoining the frontier.

5. With reference to the question of Chaman, the Amir withdraws his objection to the new British cantonment and concedes to he British Government the rights purchased by him in the Sirkai Tilerai water. At this part of the frontier the line will be drawn as follows: From the crest of the Khwaja Amran near the Psha Kotal, which remains in British territory, the line will run in such a direction as so leave Murgha Chaman and the Sharobo spring to Afghanistan, and to pass half-way between the railway station and the hill known as the Mian Baldak, and, turning south-wards, will rejoin the Khwaja Amran range, leaving the Gwasha Post in British territory, and the road to Shorawak to the west and south of Gwasha in Afghanistan. The British Government will not exercise any interference within half a mile of the road.
6. The above articles of agreement are regarded by the Government of India and His Highness the Amir of Afghanistan as a full and satisfactory settlement of all the principal differences of opinion which have arisen between them in regard to the frontier; and both the Government of India and His Highness the Amir undertake that any differences of detail, such as those which will have to be considered hereafter by the officers appointed to demarcate the boundary line, shall be settled in a friendly spirit, so as to remove for the future as far as possible all courses of doubt and misunderstanding between the two Governments. Being fully satisfied of His Highness's goodwill to the British Government, and wishing to see Afghanistan independent and strong, the Government of India will raise no objection to the purchase and import by His Highness of munitions of war, and they will themselves grant him some help in this respect. Further, in order to mark their sense of the friendly spirit in which His Highness the Amir has entered into these negotiations, the Government of India undertakes to increase by the sum of six lakhs of rupees a year the subsidy of twelve lakhs now granted to His Highness.

H.M. Durand. Amir Abdur Rahman Khan.

Appendix B
(Refers to Chapter Six)

Details of Martyrs of Battle of Saragarhi and Known Descendants

S No	*Service No.*	*Rank*	*Name*	*Father's name*	*Address Inrecords 1887-1891*	*DOB*	*M/UM*	*Details*
1	163	Sepoy	Ram Singh	Sohan Singh	Vill Kandhla, Jalandhar		UM	No Information
2	165	Havildar	Ishar Singh	Daula Singh	Vill Jhorran, Jagraon, Ludhiana	1858	M	Hav Bakhtawar Singh ex 17Sikh 4th Generation and BIkkar Singh
3	182	Sepoy	Sahib Singh					No Information
4	287	Sepoy	Ram Singh	Bragwan Singh	Vill Sadhopur, Ambala			No Information
5	332	Naik	Lal Singh	Hari Singh	Vill Dhun, Taran Taran			4th Generation Manjit Singh and Charanjit Singh
6	359	Sepoy	Hira Singh	Bara Singh	Vill Dulaowala, Lahore, Pakistan	1869	M	3rd Generation Gurmail Singh and Charan Singh
7	492	Sepoy	Uttam Singh	Lehna Singh Gill	Vill Charik, Moga, Ferozepur	1872	UM	3rd Generation Arjun Singh
8	546	Lance Naik	Chanda Singh	Ratan Singh	Vill Gaudhuan, Sunam, Sagrur	1868	M	
9	687	Sepoy	Daya Singh	Sangat Singh	Vill Kharak Singh Wala, Patiala	1870	UM	No Information
10	760	Sepoy	Jivan Singh	Hira Singh	Vill Sangatpura, Nakodar	1869	UM	No Information
11	791	Sepoy	Bhola Singh			1965	UM	No Information
12	814	Sepoy	Gurmukh Singh	Rann Singh	Vill Dhmunda, Jalandhar	1870	UM	Davinder Singh, Daljit Singh & Harprit Singh at Adampur

S No	*Service No.*	*Rank*	*Name*	*Father's name*	*Address Inrecords 1887-1891*	*DOB*	*M/UM*	*Details*
13	834	Sepoy	Narayan Singh	Gujar Singh	Vill Bassi, Patiala	1867	UM	5th Generation Arjan Singh
14	871	Sepoy	Jivan Singh	Nupa Singh	Vill Dhmunda	1869	UM	No Information
15	1221	Seopy	Nand Singh	Devi Dutta	Vill Attowal, Hoshiarpur	1873	UM	Jondjit Singh, Balbir Singh, Fateh Singh
16	1257	Sepoy	Bhagwan Singh	Hira Singh	Vill Lohgarh, Amargarh, Patiala	1872	UM	No Information
17	1265	Sepoy	Bhagwan Singh	Vir Singh	Vill Mubhewala, Ludhiana	1873	UM	No Information
18	1321	Sepoy	Sundar Singh	Sudh Singh	Vill Balia, Samrala, Ludhiana	1870	UM	No Information
19	1556	Sepoy	Buta Singh	Charat Singh	Vill Sherpur, Phillaur	1868	UM	No Information
20	1651	Sepoy	Jivan Singh	Kirpal Singh Dhariwal	Vill Guri, Phillaur	1873	UM	Mata Mohinder Kaur 3rd Generation
21	1733	Sepoy	Gurmukh Singh	Gurja Singh	Vill Chulliwal, Nokodar	1874	UM	Large Family - Mansa Singh and Jawahar Singh
22			Dadh		Vill near Samana			

Appendix C
(Refers to Chapter Six)

Photographs of Descendants and Heirs of Martyrs of Saragarhi

Paying Homage at Village Memorial Jorran of Shaheed Havildar Ishwar Singh 2016

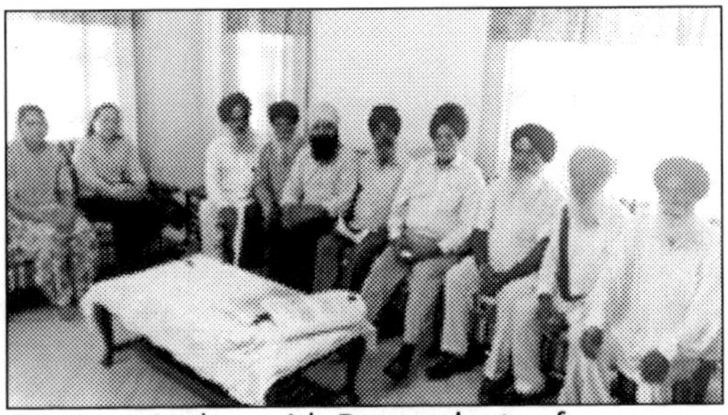
Author with Descendents of Shaheed Naik Lal Singh

Descendents of Shaheed Gurmukh Singh

Author and his wife with Descendents of Shaheed Gurmukh Singh

With Descendents of Shaheed Uttam Singh

Descendents of Shaheed Lance Naik Chanda Singh

Descendents of
Shaheed L/Nk Chanda Singh

Descendents of
Shaheed Nand Singh

Mata Mohinder Kaur, Decedents of
Shaheed Jiwan Singh

Decedents of Signalman
Gurmukh Singh

Appendix D
(Refers to Chapter Seven)

Petitions by Maliks and Elders to Amir of Cabal
07 September 1897

The British Government has been from olden times gradually encroaching upon our country, and even upon Afghan territory, and has erected forts at various points within our borders. We have complained of this to Afghan Government on many occasions, but your Highness has paid no attention to our complaints. Therefore, bring helpless, and having regard to Islam, and out constancy in religion, we have now, under the guidance of God, opened the door of jehad in the face of the said Government, and we have severed our connection with them in every way. We have plundered and destroyed five forts on the Samana above Hangu, one fort at Shinauri, at the foot of the Samana, in British territory, one fort at the Ublan Pass, near Kohat, etc., etc. There are, however, three big forts on the top of the said mountain (the Samana) which have not been taken yet. By the grace of God we will destroy and burn these also. All the people of Tirah have taken up their position on the top of the mountain (Samana); and at its base, from Kohat to the Rud-i-Kurman in the district of Kurram, the frontier of the Oraksai runs, and the tribesmen have been making jehad from time to time within their respective limits. We will never consent to tender our allegiance to the British Government, and become their subjects. We will never give up the reins of authority of our country to the hands of the Government. On the contrary, we are willing to tender our allegiance to the King of Islam. It is incumbent on the Government of Islam not only to look after our interests, and consider our position, but that of the whole of Afghanistan. We therefore send these eighteen persons from among our Maliks, Ulama and Elders, with our petitions to your Highness' presence. We are at present engaged in a jehad on the Samana range, and we request that your Highness will be pleased to do what is for our good and benefit; and, by grace of God, we will act up to your Highness' instructions,, because we leave the conduct and management of our affairs In the hands of your Highness in every respect. We have used our endeavours with our

Tribesmen to do service to your Highness. This is time to gain the object of your Highness.' All the Moslems are now at the disposal of your Highness in the shape of regular troops, artillery, and money. If the British prove victorious, they will ruin the Moslems. The services to be done on this side may be left to us by your Highness. We hope that after the perusal of our petition your Highness will favour us with a reply, dated 7 Rabius Sani, 1315 (7th September 1897).

Appendix E
(Refers to Chapter Seven)

Reply by Amir of Cabul to the Appeal of Malik
23 September, 1897

I have entered into an alliance with the British Government in regard to matters of State, and up to the present time no breach of the agreement has occurred from the side of the British, notwithstanding that they are Christians. We are Moslems and followers of the religion of the Prophet, and also of the four Khalifas of the Prophet. How can we then commit a breach of an agreement? What do you say about the verse in the Koran—"Fulfil your promise; to fulfil your promise is the first duty of a Moslem. God, on the day when the first promise was taken, asked all the creatures whether he was their God or not. They said, 'Yes, you are our God and our Creator. 'Therefore, On the day of the resurrection the first question will be about the observance of agreements. Infidels and Moslems will thus be distinguished by this test." You will thus see that the matter of the agreement is of great importance. I will never, without cause or occasion, swerve from an agreement, because the English, up to the present time, have in no way departed from the line of boundary laid down in the map they have agreed upon with me. Then why should I do so. To do so will be far from justice. I cannot, at the instance of a few interested people, bring ignominy on myself and my people.

What you have done with your own hands you must now carry on your own backs. I have nothing to do with you. You are the best judge of your affairs. Now that you have got into trouble (literally, spoiled the matter) you want me to help you. You have allowed the time when matters might have been ameliorated to slip by. Now I cannot say or do anything. I have sent back from Jellalabad the Maliks you had deputed to me. I gave them each a lungi and ten rupees for their road expenses, and I did not trouble them to come to Cabul.

I have perused your petitions, all of which were with one object. I now write to you in reply that it is eighteen years since I came to Cabul, and you know yourselves that I went to Rawal pindi (in April 1885) by the Khyber route. In consideration of my friendship with the British Government I had gone to their country as their guest, and on my way I found many of your tribesmen on both sides of the Pass, who made salaams to me. If what you state now is true, why did you not tell me at that time about the matter, so that I might here conferred with H.E. the Viceroy about it? Some years after this, when the boundary was being laid down, Sir Mortimer Durand passed through the Khyber and came to Cabul. All the frontier tribesmen knew of this, and saw the Mission with their own eyes. Why did not then your Mullahs, and Maliks, and Elders come to me when Sir Mortimer Durand come with authority to settle the boundary, so that I could have discussed the matter with him? At that time you all remained silent, and silence indicates consent. I do not know on what account now a breach has taken place between you and the English. But after you have fought them, and displeased them, you inform me.

Appendix F

(Refers to Chapter Seven)

Order of Battle of British Expeditionary Force

THE KURRAM MOVABLE COLUMN

12th [Khelat-i-Ghilzai] Regiment of Bengal Infantry.
1st Battalion, 5th Gurkha Rifles.
The Kapurthala Regiment of Imperial Service Infantry.
3rd Field Battery, Royal Artillery.
6th Regiment of Bengal Cavalry.
One Regiment of Central India Horse.
Section D of No. 3 British Field Hospital.
No. 62 Native Field Hospital.
Section b of No. 46 Native Field Hospital.
Native General Hospital, of 200 beds, at Kohat.

THE MAIN COLUMN-FIRST DIVISION

First Brigade

2nd Battalion, The Derbyshire Regiment.
1st Battalion, The Devonshire Regiment.
2nd Battalion, 1st Gurkha [Rifle] Regiment.
30th [Punjab] Regiment of Bengal Infantry.
No. 6 British Field Hospital.
No. 34 Native Field Hospital.

Second Brigade

2nd Battalion, The Yorkshire Regiment.
1st Battalion, Royal West Surrey Regiment.
2nd Battalion, 4th Gurkha [Rifle] Regiment.
3rd Regiment of Sikh Infantry, Punjab Frontier Force.
Sections A and B of No. 8 British Field Hospital.
Sections A and C of No. 14 British Field Hospital.
No. 51 Native Field Hospital.

DIVISIONAL TROOPS

No. 1 Mountain Battery, Royal Artillery.
No. 2 [Derajat] Mountain Battery.
No. 1 [Kohat] Mountain Battery.
Two Squadrons, 18th Regiment of Bengal Lancers.
28th Regiment of Bombay Infantry [Pioneers].
No. 3 Company, Bombay Sappers and Miners.
No. 4 Company, Bombay Sappers and Miners.
One Printing Section from the Bombay Sappers and Miners.
The Nabha Regiment of Imperial Service Infantry.
The Maler Kotla Imperial Service Sappers.
Sections A of No. 13 British Field Hospital.

SECOND DIVISION

Third Brigade

1st Battalion, The Gordon Highlanders.
1st Battalion, The Dorsetshire Regiment.
1st Battalion, 2nd Gurkha [Rifle] Regiment.
15th [The Ludhiana Sikh] Regiment of Bengal Infantry.
No. 24 British Field Hospital.
No. 44 Native Field Hospital.

Fourth Brigade

2nd Battalion, The King's Own Scottish Borderers.
1st Battalion, The Northamtonshire Regiment.
1st Battalion, 3rd Gurkha [Rifle] Regiment.
36th [Sikh] Regiment of Bengal Infantry.
Sections C and D of No. 9 British Hospital.
Sections A and B of No. 23 British Field Hospital.

DIVISIONAL TROOPS

No. 8 Mountain Battery, Royal Artillery.
No. 9 Mountain Battery, Royal Artillery.
No. 5 [Bombay] Mountain Battery.
Machine Gun Detachment, 16th Lancers.
Two Squadrons, 18th Regiment of Bengal Lancers.
21st Regiment of Madras Infantry [Pioneers].
No. 4 Company, Madras Sappers and Miners.
One Printing Section from the Madras Sappers and Miners.

LINE OF COMMUNICATIONS

No. 1 Kashmir Mountain Battery.
22nd [Punjab] Regiment of Bengal Infantry.
2nd Battalion, 2nd Gurkha [Rifle] Regiment.
39th [Gurhwal Rifle] Regiment of Bengal Infantry.
2nd regiment of Punjab Infantry, Punjab Frontier Force.
3rd Regiment of Bengal Cavalry.
18th Regiment, Bengal Lancers.
No. 1 Company, Bengal Sappers and Miners.
No. 42 Native Field Hospital.
No. 52 Native Field Hospital.
The Jeypore Imperial Service Transport Corps.
The Gwalior Imperial Service Transport Corps.
Ordnance Field Park.
Engineer Field Park.
British General Hospital, of 500 beds, at Rawal Pindi.
Native General Hospital, of 500 beds, at Rawal Pindi.
No. 1 Field Medical Store Depot. [For First Division.]
No. 2 Field Medical Store Depot. [For Second Division.]
No. 5 Veterinary Field Hospital.
No. 11 British Field Hospital.
No. 25 British Field Hospital.
No. 47 Native Field Hospital.
No. 64 Native Field Hospital.

THE PESHAWAR COLUMN

2nd Battalion, The Royal Innskilling Fusiliers.
2nd Battalion, The Oxfordshire Light Infantry.
9th Gurkha [Rifle] Regiment of Bengal Infantry.
34th Pioneers.
45th [Rattray's Sikh] Regiment of Bengal Infantry.
57th Field Battery, Royal Artillery.
No. 3 Mountain Battery, Royal Artillery.
9th Regiment of Bengal Lancers.
No. 5 company, Bengal Sappers and Miners.
No. 5 British Field Hospital.
No. 45 Native field Hospital, A and B Sections.
British General Hospital, of 250 beds, at Nowshera.
Native General Hospital, of 500 beds, at Nowshera

THE RAWAL PINDI RESERVE BRIGADE

2nd Battalion, The King's Own Yorkshire Light Infantry
1st Battalion, The Duke of Cornwall's Light Infantry
27th Regiment [1st Baluch Battalion] of Bombay [Light] Infantry
2nd Regiment of Infantry, Hyderabad Contingent
Jodhpur Imperial Service Lancers.
No. 12 British Field Hospital.
No. 53 Native Field Hospital.

Appendix G
(Refers to Chapter Eight)

Lieutenant Colonel John Haughton's Letters to his Wife dated 13, 15, 16 September 1897: Excerpts

"Fort Lockhart, September 13, 1897.

"Yesterday was a terrible da , for I saw twenty-one of our gallant men slaughtered at Saragarhi, and was unable to do anything to prevent it. On the 11th the General, went off with his force to save Hangu.... The situation at 9 a.m. on the 12th was as follows. The enemy were in great force on the next hill beyond Sangar (where there used to be a police post called Gogra). Another force, numbering many thousands, appeared on the hills at Saragarhi (that is, between this and Gulistan), and there were a lot more between here and Saragarhi, below the crests of the hills.... At twelve 'o' clock Saragarhi signalled that they had one sepoy killed and one Naik wounded, and three rifles broken by the enemy's bullets.... We saw the enemy make atleast two assaults on the post, but they were driven back. At three 'o' clock I came to the determination, at all costs, to try and make some diversion; so, as soon as possible afterwards, Mr. Munn and I with ninety-eight rifles went out leaving seventy-three men to defend Fort Lockhart.... We had only gone about three-quarters of a mile when we saw Saragarhi taken by the enemy. Of course it is difficult to say what occurred, but from our own observations and from reports, it seems that enemy managed to break down the door of the post (a wooden one-a fearful mistake), and then our poor men ran down from the parapet to defend the doorway.

"September 15, 1897.

Major Des Voeux, who was surrounded at Gulistan, saw the Pathans at Saragarhi making a hole in a dead angle in the wall. They got in there, and our men ran down to defend the hole, and the enemy immediately swarmed over the walls. The end was not long, though it is said that one poor fellow defended himself in the guard-room and shot twenty of the enemy inside the post. The brutes then set the place on fire. Meanwhile

Gulistan was being attacked, and, after the fall of Saragarhi, its captors went off to help the Pathans at Gulistan, leaving some thousands at Saragarhi to prevent succour going to Gulistan.... The next morning things were very critical, and Major Des Voeux gave leave to a Havildar and sixteen men, who had volunteered, to make a sortie.... They were having a bad time of it, when another Havildar and eleven man got over the end of the hornwork and went to their aid. This turned the scale and the gallant little party drove the enemy back at this point and took three of their standards.... I regret to say that of the two Havildars one is already dead, and the other, I fear, cannot live. The sortie had a wonderfully depressing effect on the enemy, and a splendid effect on all our men....

"September 16, 1897

In thousand at Saragarhi and possibly nearer which meant that day would at any rate be nearer Fort Lockhart than i should be when I went out to meet the general, I gave up the plan for the time. However, at about seven 'o' clock Mr. Munn, with thirty of our men and about a dozen of the Royal Irish went out and got down to a bit of hill below Sangar, where we were able to get some good though long-range volleys into the enemy as they retired before the General. They did not make much resistance directly they heard the guns. I cannot say what damage our volleys did to them, as they were so scattered about over the hillside, but we could see our bullets going all in among them and knocking up the dust. About those same guns (of Captain Parkers mountain battery), they had gone up the Kurram with Colonel Richardson's column, but when the general found they were more wanted here than there they marched back seventy-two miles in seventy hours then, after a day's rest, they came on with general from Hangu to Gulistan. Well to continue: as soon as the enemy had fled from their position Sangar, the general said he must push on hard to Gulistan. So we with our few men raced back to Fort Lockhart, got all the men we had left there out, and, without asking permission, stuck our ourselves at the head of General's force. Poor Saragarhi was absolutely a heap of stones, but amongst the ruins we could distinguish the remains of our poor fellows, hacked to pieces by these fiends.... Then, when we got beyond the Saragarhi heights and could see Gulistan, we saw the enemy as thick as peas round it; but they bolted like French partridges as soon as we showed our noses a mile and a half off, and, unfortunately, it was long time before the guns could get up. When the did get up there were very few of the enemy left within range; and though the guns opened a pretty accurate fire, I don't fancy the enemy could have could have suffered much. We found our people at Gulistan very cheery. The general is awfully pleased with all our men; I think they have just done spandidly. Mrs. Des Voeux is wonderful; she had had pretty high fever, but the morning of our arrival her temperature was normal. She was very cheerful , and looked wonderfully well. Teresa has just been splendid,* nursing the world, etc.

"I am sorry to say, out of the garrison of 121 there were forty-one wounded (not counting those wounded before), many of them very severely. Several have since died, and I fear more will die. Dr. Prall worked like a horse, or like a whole team of horses. Major Des Voeux reports that Mr. Pratt did splendidly. I hope he and Major Des Voeux and Dr. Prall will be well rewarded.

Appendix H

(Refers to Chapter Eight)

Excerpts of Letter Written by Lt Col J Haughton to General Sir Charles Gough, VC, GCB etc: Camp Mamanai

January 16, 1898

...Having been on the Samana among the Orkazais for a year, I had perhaps more opportunities of forming an opinion than many others. I don't think the present disturbances can be put down to any cause, and myself I do not think the so called 'forward policy' is mainly responsible. There is no doubt that, amongst other causes, the Greek defeat by the Turks had a good deal of effect, and was used by unscrupulous persons to stir up disquiet. From letters found in Mullah's house in Tirah, it appeared that the Afridis believed, or at any rate were told, that the English had been beaten by the Turks – that the Russians also had gone against us, and that Suez Canal was blocked, and we could not get any troops through. I believe myself that, without any direct action, our friend, the Amir was not sorry that we should have a thorn in our sides, and also not sorry that Afridis should get punishment for not having responded to his claim to be their suzerain, and consequently he connived at their being egged on by the Afghans, notably by the Sipah-Salar. Although the Afridis and Orakazais are not particularly religious, and have themselves said that the tales spread by the Mullahs are all "Mullayani durogh" i.e. Mullahs' lies, yet, given any feeling of disquiet, the elder men cannot withstand the Mullahs, backed by the young blood who are generally spoiling for a fight.... I do not think the Orakazais, or at any rate greater part of them, ever had their hearts in it, but were dragged by the Mullahs and by the Afridis. On the Samana we only had half a battalion distributed in seven posts spreading along eight miles of crest. Nevertheless, if we had had a couple of mountain guns, we could not only have completely held our own, but thrashed the enemy had they come on the Samana, which I doubt whether they could have done, Saragarhi, certainly, was a rotten little post, but I must confess that I did not expect it to be regularly attacked in the way it was, as I did not think the enemy would consider its capture worth the great loss they were bound to and did suffer. A great deal has been said about Saragarhi, and, as far as pluck goes, no one could have done more than the poor fellows who fought to the last gasp; but, personally, I think much more highly of the sortie from Gulistan, which was worthy of the best traditions of the Sikhs and of the Indian Army. ...I consider every one of the sortie party should have got the order of merit, and that as soon as possible....

The astonishing and blood-curdling accounts that one sees in some of the home papers would be very amusing, if one did not know that they made one's people at home anxious. ...the native troops and the Indian Generals have certainly shown up well on all occasion.... But thanks to the guerilla tactics of the enemy, and their being so well armed(especially Lee-Metfords taken from the British troops) our losses have been out of all proportions to the amount actual fighting; but it is difficult to see how this could have been avoided.... Now the enemy, with Lee-Metfords and smokeless powder, make it very uncomfortable in the valley from tops of hills up to eighteen hundred yards on either side; as we could not see them, and, thanks to the smokeless powder, could not even see where they were, neither our rifle nor artillery fire could do much against scattered small groups.... The work of the advanced and rear guards was enormous, and the enemy, being as active as cats and knowing he ground, enabled a few men with magazine rifles to make it very hot for any party coming to crown a height; and, of course, by the time the party got to the top, with possibly several casualties, not a sign of the enemy was to be seen, till a vicious "phit-phit" or two of a Lee-Metford told you he was on another height half a mile away....

Yours Sincerely,

J. Haughton

Appendix J
(Refers to Chapter Thirteen)

Battle and Theatre Honours and Appreciations of 4 Sikh: 1887 to 2018

Battle Honours

Manipur 1891
Samana 1897
Tihar 1897-98
Saragarhi 1897
Tsing Tao 1914
Hai 1917
Omars 1941
Agoroat 1941
Karen 1941
Abyssinia 1941
Dier-El-Shein 1941
Gothic Line 1944
Monte Clavo 1944
San Marino 1945
Barki 1965
Sirmani 1971

Theatre Honours

Assam 1891
Punjab Frontier 1897-98
China 1914
Mesopotamia 1917
Persia 1917-18
Abyssinia 1940-41
Italy 1943-45
Punjab 1965
East Pakistan 1971

Appreciations

Force Commanders UNIFIL Unit Citation
GOC-in-C Western Command Unit Citation

Appendix K

(Refers to Chapter Thirteen)

Honours and Awards 4 Sikh Till 2018

Pre-Independence		*Post-Independence*	
MC	12	MVC	02
CBE	01	VrC	08
OBE	01	SC	01
OSI	01	AVSM	01
DSO	05	VSM	01
IOM	74	SM	11
IDSM	37	COAS Commendation Cards	13
Mention in Despatches	45	Vice COAS Commendation Cards	01
Commendation Cards	01	Army Cdr's Commendation Cards	22
McGregor Medal	01	Force Cdr's Commendation Cards	81
Serbian Decorations	04		
Russian Decorations	03		
Romanian Decorations	03		
Italian Decorations	01		
Jubilee Medals	25		
Coronation Medals	20		
IMSM	02		

Appendix L
(Refers to Chapter Fourteen)

From The Pioneer Allahabad: 30 January 1899 Regarding Brave End of Lt Col J Haughton at Shinkamar

Five miles to West we saw the spreading jaws
Of that dead defile, Shinkamar's dark pass,
Wither at dawn of day of the little band,
Four hundred hardy dalesmen, Yorkshire's best,
And half their tail of Sikhs, the Khalsa's pride,
Threaded their rocky way.
'Twas now full noon, And in the busy camp slow whispers passed.
"They marched at five, they should be back by one.
What is the last message? Is there any news? What says the General?"
So the day wore on. Lining the wall, we stood with straining eyes,
And each man asked his fellow what he saw.
Then came the distant helio's fitful flash: "Entangled in the nullah-can't get out;
Cumbered with wounded, and they press us close;
We hold our own, but hardly-send us help."
Sudden the bugle blared, the camp uprose,
To arms the Borderer and the Gurkha sprang,
And he, their leader in forty fights,
First in attack and rearmost in retreat, Led now the way.
Too late, alas! Too late!
Scarce had the common rallying-point been reached,
When the curt message, flag sent, came to hand,
And silent men learnt how John Haughton died.
"Someone had blundered," and the keen eye foe,
Quick to attain the vantage-point in flank,
Pressed on, a hidden host.
With grim intent The veteran Sikh the oft-fought fight renewed,
The stubborn Tyke in dogged silence met his baptism of fire.
Still undismayed. The rear-guard stood, for Haughton bade them stand,

And Haughton's voice to each fresh courage gave,
And Haughton's heart each doubtful breast inspired.
And Haughton's self ten times a hero proved.
Vain the attempt!
Swarming on every side, With hard-won rifle and with rude jezail,
From every rock the howling tribesmen poured.
Swift came the end.
'Twas thus that Haughton died,
And with him Turing, standing by his chief.
But not in vain: respite by the stand.
Sowly and wearily the column reached
The open plain and safety, and the foe.
Balked of their savage lust, turned to the spoil.
So died John Haughton: by the camp fire's gleam
White men and black their common grief outpoured,
England had lost a hero: Sikhs their chief;
The camp its genius; each all and a friend.
But though our loss struck deeply, what of them?
The widow war-bereft, the orphaned son.
The unseen babe-unseen but not unloved;
We thought of them; and every man was dumb.

Appendix M

(Refers to Chapter Fourteen)

Personal Account of an Officer on Visit to Samana in 1997

A Retired historian officer, Major (Retd) Muhammad Nawaz Khan, 5FF, residing in Peshawar, visited Samana Ridge on the Centenary of the Battle of Saragarhi. His related words are given here in excerpts:

> *"It was on 17th June, that I drove for over 125 Kilometers from Peshawar to Samana, via Kohat and Hangu...the first monument that I saw was a commemorative memorial...the "Saragarhi Memorial 1897". It is in perfect condition, which may be because the Orakzai tribesmen also want to keep the memory of their action alive. There is a plaque fixed on one side, which gives the details of the Saragarhi action. The memorial is about twenty feet high. In fact, it could be twenty-one feet because the British at times did indulge in such novelties.*
>
> *....close by, the formidable Fort Lockhart and then drove towards Saragarhi village. The village is located at a lower place and the communication post (for Helios) had to be at a higher point....I walked up on the abandoned track, which is about 8 feet wide, with trees grown over it. I proceeded further up through boulders and bushes and reached the top. There, I saw a heap of loose stones. I went towards it and found that the stones were all dressed. It was a pleasant surprise to see the base wall intact. This was the moment of my dreams, the famous Saragarhi communication Post, built in 1891 and destroyed in 1897. The base of the post is intact with dressed stones and cement. It was made twelve feet square at a height of about six feet. The walls tapered inwards at about 85 degrees. The debris suggests that the post could have been about 12 feet high. Close to this site, there was a 12 feet square enclosure, with a small entrance. It could have been a place for guards. Slightly below was a big enclosure, probably meant for bivouacs. I saw the area around and found this spot on the ridge to be the right place for a post because, from here, Fort Lockhart and Fort Gulistan could be connected in those days. I picked up a few pieces of dressed stones as souvenirs and left. One hundred years had not changed the Samana Ridge and the Valiant Orakzais."*

Appendix N

(Refers to Chapter Fourteen)

Contributions by Brig Kanwaljit Singh Veteran (Author)

Paintings for 4 Sikh and Ferozepur Memorial Gurudawara: 1987

Book 'Ashes to Glory - The Saragarhi Battalion' released on Centenary of 4 Sikh Raising Day: 1987

Constructed at Sikh Regimental Center, Ramgarh, in December 1991

Mobile Memorial in 4 Sikh Made in 1987

Museum and Motivation Hall Constructed 1993-1995,at the Sikh Regimental Center Ramgarh (Author with Staff in the Picture)

Appendix O
(Refers to Chapter Fourteen)

Present Day Pictures of Samana

Samana

Saragarhi Plinth

Ruins of Cairn

Saragarhi Area

Fort Lockhart

Way to Saragarhi Memorial at Samana

(From the books of Captain Amarinder Singh and Mr G S Josan)

Appendix P

Location at Samana from Google Map

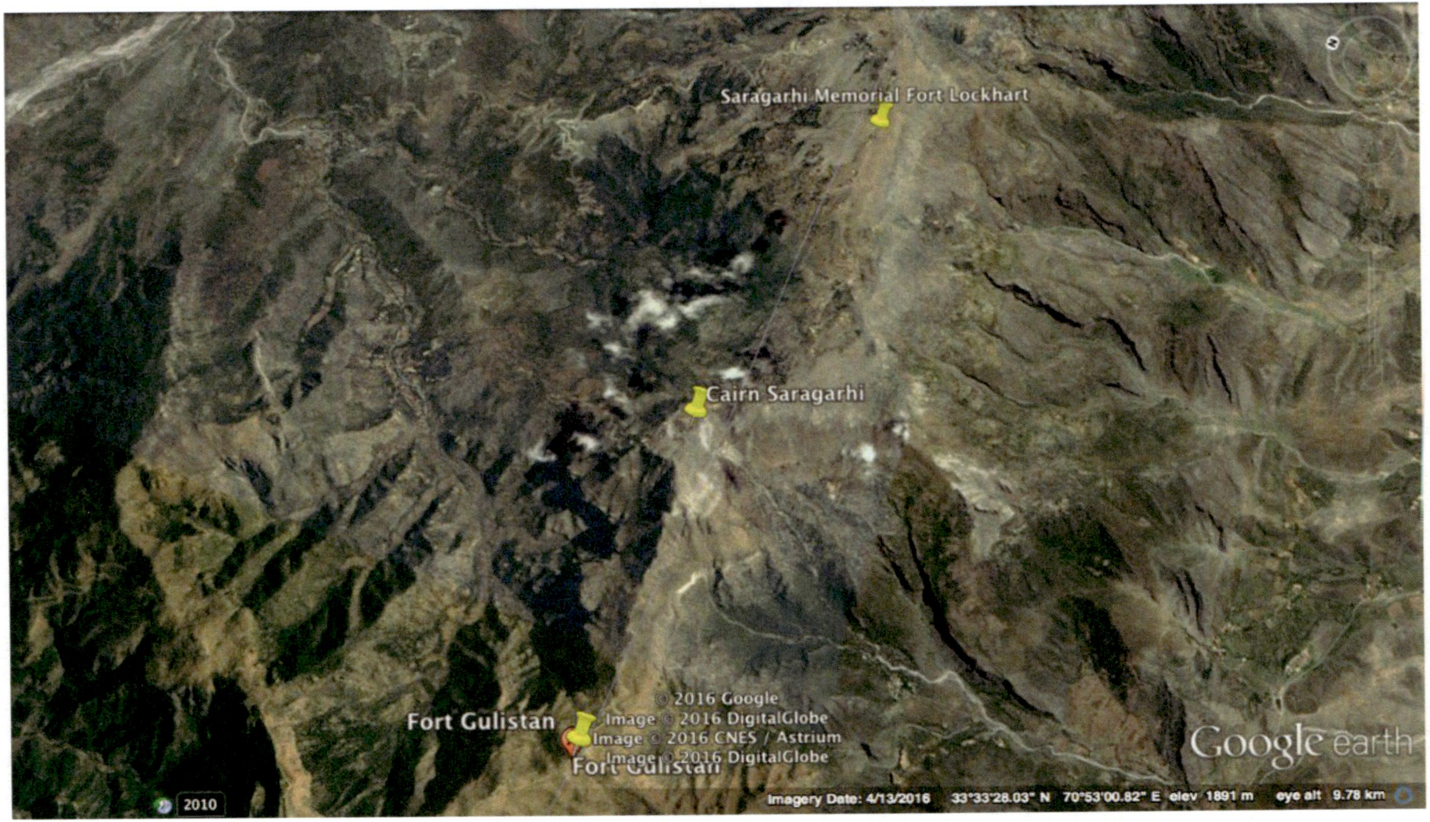

Bibliography

1. The 36th Sikhs Digest of Service Vol 1: 1887-1913.
2. The Saragarhi Battalion – Ashes to Glory by Colonel Kanwaljit Singh and Major H S Ahluwalia.
3. Presentation Battle of Saragarhi by 4 Sikh.
4. The Tirah Campaign Vols 1 and 2 by Colonel H C Hutchison.
5. The 1897 Revolt and Tirah Valley Operations from the Pashtun Perspective by Robert A Johnson (Tribal Analysis Centre).
6. Lieutenant Colonel John Haughton by Major A C Yate.
7. The Frontier 1839-1947 by Major J G Elliot.
8. Campaign on the North-West Frontier by Captain H L Nevill DSO.
9. The Frontier Ablaze: The North-West Frontier Rising 1897-98 by Michael Barthorp.
10. Afghanistan North West Frontier by Michael E Lambart.
11. The Malakand Field Force by Winston Churchill.
12. Tirah by T H Holdich (Geographical Journal).
13. The Indian Frontier War by Lionel James.
14. The Army in India and Development of Frontier Warfare 1849-1947 by T R Moreman.
15. The Pathan Revolt in North West India by H Woonam Mills.

16. 'Punjabisation' in the British Indian Army 1857-1947 and the Advent of Military Rule in Pakistan by Sayed Hussain Shaheed Soharwardi.

17. A Legacy of Valour – The Sikh Regiment.

18. Punjab State War Heroes Memorial and Mueum – Inaugural Coffee Table Book – Director, Directorate of Defence Services Welfare, Punjab, Series Edited by Major General Raj Mehta, AVSM, VSM.

19. Ranjit Singh – Maharaja of the Punjab by Khushwant Singh.

20. The Sikhs and the Sikh Wars by Gen Sir, Charles Gough, VC, GCB, and Arthur D Innes, MA.

21. The Rise, Conquest and Annexation of the Punjab State by Gen Sir, Charles Gough, VC, GCB, Arthur D Innes, MA.

22. The Sikh Regiment in the Second World War by Colonel F T Birdwood.

23. Indian Army by Major Donovan Jackson.

24. Saragarhi and the Defence of the Samana Forts - The 36th Sikhs in the Tirah Campaign 1897-98 by Amarinder Singh.

25. A Saga of Valour - The Epic Battle of Saragarthi by Gurinderpal Singh Josan.

Note: Numerous articles researched to analyse all possible angles about the countries, lands, people, leaders, battles, expeditions, campaign, outcome, other great battles, war cries, why soldiers fight, commemorations and what more. Though of great use and value, listing is avoided.

Index